T0197328

# UNWARP
# The
# MIRROR

## Clearly Seeing God's Grace

ALMA & REV. RANDALL FORBES

WESTBOW
PRESS®
A DIVISION OF THOMAS NELSON
& ZONDERVAN

WestBow Press books may be ordered through booksellers or by contacting:

WestBow Press
A Division of Thomas Nelson & Zondervan
1663 Liberty Drive
Bloomington, IN 47403
www.westbowpress.com
844-714-3454

ISBN: 978-1-6642-2489-6 (sc)
ISBN: 978-1-6642-2490-2 (e)

Print information available on the last page.

WestBow Press rev. date: 02/26/2021

# WAY TO GO, ALMA!

Alma's dream has long been to reach out to those women who have not found the grace they so desperately need and long for. It is not from God they seek it as much as from their fellow people. God's grace is always available; grace from other people is harder to come by.

We both have desired to help men and women understand their responsibility as Christians—to extend the grace of God as they can, show compassion and love to their fellow travelers in this life, and accept a repentant heart into the family, as God accepts them.

Should we not be the first sign of grace a person finds when they enter the doors of the church? Should the lost not find love and grace in the children of God as they come close to the Lord? If they should, then why do they not? Too many times, Alma and I have encountered people, mostly women, who have come to find peace and joy in the Lord, only to be met with judgment and condemnation by people.

No, this does not always happen, but it does all too frequently. Too many people claim to be children of God yet refuse to act like Christ with compassion and love.

It has been an uphill struggle for Alma as she has fought traditions, social stigmas, and rude behavior from those who should know better. But she has persevered in this frontier as she prepared the way for so many others to find grace among the true children of God.

I commend Alma for her determination to find the truth about our Lord and the fruit of His Spirit—love, joy, peace, patience, kindness, goodness, faithfulness, gentleness, and self-control in those who are His. May she be blessed as she blesses others.

With all my love,
Randy

# Transition 1

## Into the Story:
### The Choice to Look into This Mirror

The more elegant lettering of the Times New Roman font is what Alma uses to share what she has on her heart.

**The bold, simple Arial font indicates Randy's pastoral input.**

Scripture quotations are from the New International Version of the Holy Bible.

# ALMA'S STORY

It might have been a sunny day many years ago; I honestly do not recall. I do remember how gloomy it quickly became as the day unfolded, and I found out that I was pregnant.

I do recall how darkness crept into my life as though Satan had come to grab my heart and steal my life away.

I immediately felt overwhelmed, full of despair, and angry with myself for getting into this situation. There was a feeling of disbelief and shock; I believed it could not happen to me—what a teenage lie! Sick to my stomach, I did not know which way to turn. I felt all alone. My world completely changed. Suddenly, it was a very scary and uncomfortable place. I was being forced to grow up and make adult decisions quickly—too quickly, I might add!

Major decisions had to be made, and what started with a bad choice continued on to more bad choices. Should my parents be involved? I already felt enough self-hatred without adding to it.

Desperately needing a place to talk, I contacted a friend who was very sympathetic to my situation. She asked what I wanted to do about it, and having an abortion would soon become my solution. We called the father of the child and informed him. We then began making the required arrangements to "solve the problem."

I felt that carrying this child to term would be like signing my whole life away, and I was not ready for that or for the responsibility that went along with having a child.

Feelings of guilt and shame for getting into this mess were there from the beginning. My situation, my solution, my fears, and my anger with myself consumed every moment of every day. I cannot say that any thoughts were rational or made any sense. All I knew was that it would soon be over, and I could continue on with my life as I had known it—or so I thought.

Years passed, many of them—too many and not very easy ones. Years of guilt and shame. Years of regret and hopelessness. I had a specific cupboard in my kitchen where I kept my broom and vacuum, along with a few other things. Every time I opened that cupboard door, for some reason, I would think of the skeleton in my closet that I was hiding and feeling guilty about. My cupboard was just about as tall as I was, and my short, little skeleton body would have fit in there just about perfectly—along, of course, with my large, overloaded soul of sins. I often took my frustrations and anger out on the cupboard, with the door being slammed or some grunting going on—quite frequently, I might add.

My anger often overflowed and came out toward things in my home and, unfortunately, occasionally toward some people. I struggled with anger with myself and lashed out at others. It seems, however, that all humankind has skeletons in its closets; some people are just very good at concealing them.

Trying to maintain a "perfect" image of who I was turned out to be an unending and unattainable chore—and very unrewarding. The only person I was fooling was myself.

I had accepted Jesus Christ as my Savior after this incident in my life, the abortion. It was also after I was married and had children. When I accepted Christ, I repented of my sins, I asked for forgiveness, and I asked Jesus to live in me and through me.

As the years went by, I realized that laying my sins at His feet was a process. I lay more and more at His feet as time passed—easier ones at first, then progressing to the tougher ones. This big one was one of the last.

Looking in the mirror was very difficult for me because I no longer liked what I saw within or outside myself. I was afraid of what I would see in the mirror of my soul. There was nothing beautiful anymore. I had destroyed all that with the abortion.

I was also afraid to read God's Word for fear of the condemnation I expected to find. I feared sinking even deeper into the mire of depression. For years, I had neglected God's Word and also left God's amazing grace undiscovered.

As I fought to appear perfect in this world, I relegated myself to just being a sinner saved by Jesus. That is how I dealt with the abortion; I put it aside.

Reading His Word, which we are instructed to do, clearly tells us that His grace is sufficient. There is no other way but through Jesus Christ.

This journey has enabled me to look at myself in the mirror once again but through the eyes of God. I have found God's matchless grace, mercy, and love.

Through the tender loving care of Jesus, I eventually was able to lay that at His feet as well. The tensions of life became fewer, the weight was a lot lighter, and the battle was no longer fought because Jesus was victorious over it. What a relief!

Here are some questions, for those readers who find themselves in similar situations mine, that may help you go back and retrace your steps to find your story. From there, maybe you can move forward:

Why did you have sex to begin with? (That's another topic entirely.)

What was your response to finding out you were pregnant?

Did you immediately think of having an abortion?

Did you feel that it would answer all the problems and the mess you got yourself into?

Did you approach your parents?

There may be different questions we each have to answer. Maybe we just need to answer the questions we've been avoiding for so long before we can go on. You decide for yourself. Maybe think about these questions and then continue.

**Why Did I Write?**

God gave me a picture of fields and fields of women who have had abortions and cannot live victorious lives. There is victory in Jesus!

I was compelled—strongly moved by God—to write this book

to help women who have had abortions find forgiveness in God's grace, so they can find freedom in Christ and live and share their freedom with others.

May we who believe in Christ find strength to show God's grace as well, and may our churches open their doors to all who need God's grace.

## The Pivotal Point

The pivotal point of this book is the cross *of* Christ and the cost *to* Christ.

It is about some of the wrong choices we make in life, realizing the need for the cross because of our sin, finding freedom, and, finally, loving the cross and desiring to serve the one who died on the cross.

To me, there is no other way to rise above issues in our lives than through Jesus Christ, who is "the Way, the Truth and the Life" (John 14: 6). The only catch is that God wants the glory, and we must give it to Him through the acknowledgement of who He is—God Almighty—and what He is capable of doing if we allow Him .

Before I decided to write this book, God allowed me to meet some of the women who had chosen an abortion- those fields of women again. If you are one of them, you are not alone, even though you may feel very much alone.

As for the babies, Jesus is standing in the middle of a field of babies, as big as the field of women, and He loves each one. And Jesus's love does not stop there; it overflows and shines on us. We can claim it.

Not everyone who has had an abortion or was involved in one believes that abortion is wrong, as they are entitled. This book is for those who do believe it is wrong and want forgiveness from the Lord.

If you are not at the cross yet, perhaps this book can help you get there. If you are at the cross but stuck, perhaps it will help you move forward. If you have been at the cross and have moved on, perhaps we can help you reach out to those around you who need your help.

# SECTION I

# GETTING TO THE CROSS

## THE FIRST CHOICE:
# INITIAL CHOICE

It amazes me that God allows us our free will and where we go with it. He never forces Himself on us, but He uses the situations we have managed to get ourselves into to bring us to Him. We can take no credit for receiving forgiveness and being accepted by God as His children, nor do we have any valid reason to blame Him for any of our actions and decisions.

The topic of creating a baby was never one I discussed with anyone. I did not have sex with the intention of having a baby or creating a human being. Pregnancy was a result of having sex.

Have you lived with a choice you should not have made?

Have you ever made a choice you wish you could change? Often, that choice, whether good or bad, is the result of a series of other choices. The choice we remember often is the last choice in a run of choices—the straw that broke the camel's back. Often, they are all similar—good choices follow good choices, and bad ones follow other bad ones.

In the next chapter, we'll talk about the choice of abortion that is a major issue in the lives of all the parties involved. There, we'll trace back to the first choice that led to the series of choices that resulted in that monumental decision, which seemed necessary.

This discussion may be redundant at this point in your life but may be a preventative in someone else's life. Or this discussion may be a necessary part of healing from a bad choice. Either way, we'll attempt to lead to what initiated the series of events and decisions made.

In short, the abortion was the resulting decision of an unwanted pregnancy; the pregnancy may have been the result of a decision to have unprotected sex, and so on.

There are times, of course, when unwanted pregnancies are the result of other events, such as rape, but we'll concentrate on those that are the result of a decision to have unprotected sex or where the protection was inadequate.

The initial decision was to have sex without wanting to have children. This can happen in or out of marriage. Within a marriage, the decision to have a sexual relationship without wanting children is a legitimate one but one that would also necessitate protection against pregnancy.

Outside of marriage, a sexual relationship is against the will of God, and therefore, it's the initial decision that I am considering here. Whether the decision was to have sex outside of marriage or to have unprotected sex within a marriage, each decision has good or bad consequences.

Whenever there is a decision to have sex, there is a risk of pregnancy. Whenever there is a decision not to have sex, there is no chance of pregnancy. This initial decision is the one that necessitates the other decisions. Often, one decision is the result or consequence of another.

Sometimes the decision to do nothing is the wrong decision. Deciding not to remove oneself from a situation may result in a decision to participate in an activity that becomes detrimental. One thing leads to another.

Initial decisions are critical to success in many different aspects of life. Life truly is one step at a time, and that can be a step in the right direction or the wrong direction.

Let's follow the course of two decisions. First, let's follow the course discussed in this book. The first decision is made to have sex with an interesting person. This encounter may or may not be a protected event. In any case, it possibly will become an unprotected event at some point, whether by decision or by accidental equipment failure. Either way, a decision is made that leads to pregnancy.

A subsequent decision to abort the pregnancy is not the first or only choice that leads to abortion. It follows the others I just mentioned.

Now let's look at the other course that is possible. The first choice is to abstain from having sex. This leads to the absolute impossibility of equipment failure and no need whatsoever for another decision about protection. The outcome does not and cannot include pregnancy and leaves no requirement for a decision about abortion.

In this case, the first decision eliminates the need for any of the others and also eliminates the potential consequences.

A lot of other scenarios are possible; these two are only the basics. I present them here to make the point that we need to trace back to the original decision before we condemn ourselves for one big, bad one made along the way.

The outcome is what we must deal with in the end. How we got there may not seem important, but it shows us that the outcome is rarely the result of one final, catastrophic decision.

We tend to fixate on our pasts just far enough to take in our last big sin, and we get hooked on it. It was years before I could look beyond the abortion to see what led me to that outcome in the first place. It took just as long to see that I was a sinner before my abortion and before the first choice.

Maybe the reason we just look at our last big sins is because we are told they are the only ones we should be concerned with. They are the sins that attract the attention of others. Our heavenly Father sees sin as sin, and He views all humankind the same—as sinners. We cannot allow ourselves to stay focused on the big ones only. In order to move on, we need to remember who we are dealing with— God, not people.

Regardless of the choices we make, there are consequences, some good and some not so good. Sometimes, the subsequent decisions are part of the consequences of a former decision.

Choose to keep your focus on God and what He says and promises. Allow yourself to believe what God says: "'For my thoughts are not your thoughts, neither are your ways my ways,' declares the LORD" (Isaiah 55:8). In doing so, you will move forward. Be open to His ways and thoughts.

Now, don't get too down on yourself for the bad decisions you may have made in life. They are common and survivable. There is a light at the end of the tunnel. There is hope, even for the worst situation. Keep reading. When you get to the part about remorse, you will start to understand for yourself, if you don't already.

THE SECOND CHOICE:

# CONSEQUENTIAL CHOICE

The choice to abort an unwanted pregnancy is a devastating decision for many women. It is promoted as a birth control option, much like the pill is promoted as a birth control option. It is also a choice that could be avoided.

We tend to fixate on abortion as the crucial choice, but it is, in fact, the second or a subsequent choice we have made. The first choice was to have sex without considering pregnancy, usually outside of marriage.

Other choices along the way may have led here, but let's call it the second choice for simplicity. Choices, whether first, second, or subsequent, are influenced by opinions and beliefs.

Some people have different opinions or beliefs about when the fetus is considered an individual human being. I now base my decision on God's Word: "For you created my inmost being; you knit me together in my mother's womb" (Psalm 139:13). To my understanding, the moment the DNA connected together, God's hand was there, busily creating a human form. For me, there is no argument; the human form is in the image of God, created by God, and made as an individual from the instant of conception. I did not believe this at the time.

That term *knit* has been used in the description of the conception action of DNA. When the male and female DNA string halves connect with each other, they form a new and complete DNA imprint of the new person. I suppose that would also mean that the DNA of the new person is not the same as that of the mother or father, therefore making the person a separate but dependent individual.

Often, there are other outside influences to decision-making as well. Sometimes, the father of the child insists on an abortion. Sometimes, a parent or guardian demands putting the child up for adoption. Sometimes, medical personnel innocently refer to the unwanted pregnancy as a "problem" that they can "help you take care of." These and more can influence any decision regarding the child.

These other individuals are not innocent of influence; they are responsible for their input as much as we are responsible for our decisions. We must realize we cannot take responsibility for their parts, nor can we make them responsible for ours.

Another significant influence is God.

Initially, I did pray to God, even in my unbelief. When things go wrong, it is strange that we automatically turn to God for help. I can still remember crying out to God with my unbeliever's prayer: "Oh my, what have I gotten myself into, God? Help me get out of this one, *please.*"

Have you ever been there? Have you ever found yourself in a place where you could not see a way out? Have you been where only God could help you because there was no other way?

I call it the unbeliever's prayer because it is usually where an unbeliever becomes a believer. It is the place in people's lives where they run out of their own resources and call on God, even if they only have a twinkling of faith in Him.

What an awesome place it was when I ran out of myself and was forced to turn to God. I was asking for an answer that would be more like a miracle, "Please turn back time so I'm not in this situation, so I don't have to make this decision." It was too late for that but not too late for God to be involved, even though I didn't fully understand that yet.

God's involvement is always for our greater good, even if it seems impossible at first. We may not always do as He directs—in fact, we often still follow our own foolishness—but we can acknowledge that God is there and that we want His input.

Alma has often referred to King David in this way: "David—a man after God's own heart." Here's why:

Second Samuel 11 tells the story of David and Bathsheba. It is the classic example of a man lusting after a married woman. The first five verses explain how this happens and that Bathsheba ends up pregnant. Verses 6 to 13 show David trying and failing to get the husband, Uriah, to lie with his wife to hide the adultery. Verses 14 to 27 describe how King David finally has Uriah killed in war, which frees David and Bathsheba to marry.

The very end of this chapter tells how God felt about the matter taking place: "But the thing that David had done displeased the LORD" (2 Samuel 11: 27b).

David actually made a series of second wrong choices. He kept going from one bad move to another until he was in very deep—and God was not pleased with this. David seemed to not see beyond his own selfish desires; he couldn't see what he was doing to the lives of others.

Second Samuel 12 brings the story to a more fitting close.

God sends the prophet Nathan to King David to bring a message from the Lord. The message is brought in the form of a parable. Nathan tells David:

> There were two men in a certain town, one rich and the other poor. The rich man had a very large number of sheep and cattle, but the poor man had nothing except one little ewe lamb he had bought. He raised it, and it grew up with him and his children. It shared his food, drank from his cup and even slept in his arms. It was like a daughter to him.
>
> Now a traveler came to the rich man, but the rich man refrained from taking one of his own sheep or cattle to prepare a meal for the traveler who had come to him. Instead he took the ewe lamb that belonged to the poor man and prepared it for the one who had come to him. (2 Samuel 12:1–4)

King David did not get the hint, so Nathan told him a little more bluntly what God was trying to say.

> David burned with anger against the man and said to Nathan, "As surely as the LORD lives, the man who did this deserves to die! He must pay for that lamb four times over, because he did such a thing and had no pity.
> Then Nathan said to David, "You are the man ..." 2 Samuel 12:5–7)

God knew what David had done and confronted him on it through Nathan.

> Then David said to Nathan, "I have sinned against the LORD."
> Nathan replied, "The LORD has taken away your sin. You are not going to die." (2 Samuel 12:13)

The story goes on to tell how the child died and what David did then:

> Then David comforted his wife Bathsheba, and he went to her and lay with her. She gave birth to a son, and they named him Solomon. The LORD loved him. (2 Samuel 12:24)

The Lord loved the child of David and Bathsheba. The Lord also loved David. David repented of his sin and then did what he believed was the best thing to do: he took care of those he had wronged.

Many times, David made mistakes—sometimes big ones—and then had to face the Lord. God loved him through all of them. Even though David was a king, he was just a man with a special job.

Later, David gained a reputation of being loved greatly by the Lord.

He testified concerning him: "I have found David
the son of Jesse a man after my own heart; he will
do everything I want him to do." (Acts 13:22)

Even though David is referred to as a man after God's own
heart, he could still stray from what pleased God in his personal life.
God gave David to the people of Israel as their king because he was
searching after the heart of God.

Isn't it moving that David—who had an affair with a married
woman he lusted after; who got her pregnant and plotted to have her
husband killed—could still be considered a man after God's heart?
Amazing!

We too are loved by our God to that same extent. I was moved
by these passages in the Bible because, as many of the stories in the
Bible show, God deals with normal, sinful people. We are all in need
of His touch and His healing.

Repentance can move mountains and stir God's heart for us. If
David, who was simply a man, could be forgiven, surely God can
forgive me.

God did not hold the mistakes against David because David's
heart belonged to God. Even though David messed up, he was
willing to look at himself and change what was necessary. He would
admit his mistakes, his sins, and move on.

Sometimes we make mistakes, even big ones, and have to
repent and do what is best. We must take care of the mess we have
made, if possible. Even though we mess up, if we are willing to be
corrected or admit our mistakes and do better, then we are people
after God's own heart as well.

David jumped from one bad choice to another in his story with
Bathsheba, but he repented when he knew he had done wrong. No
matter how far we go before being caught or catching ourselves, we
can turn back.

David still had to suffer the consequences of his actions, but he
could remain in the will of God while doing it.

If we do not rebel against God, and we obey His commands, we
too can be known as someone after God's own heart. Regardless

of the choices we make, we can be devoted to God. He is God. He is the God of second chances, as we see in His teachings to us:

> Then Peter came to Jesus and asked, "Lord, how many times shall I forgive my brother when he sins against me? Up to seven times?" Jesus answered, "I tell you, not seven times, but seventy times seven." (Matthew 18: 21–22)

> If he sins against you seven times in a day, and seven times comes back to you and says, "I repent," forgive him. (Luke 17:4)

This means we must be willing to forgive an unlimited number of times. Jesus taught us to forgive the way He forgives us. We are given second chances and are asked to give second chances to all who need them—like women who have had abortions, have repented, and need a second chance; we need to give them a second chance.

David sang of his repentance, his rejoicing in the Lord, and the Lord's forgiveness. This one helped Alma move on from a place where she was stuck.

For the director of music. A psalm of David. When the prophet Nathan came to him after David had committed adultery with Bathsheba.

> Have mercy on me, O God,
> according to your unfailing love;
> according to your great compassion
> blot out my transgressions.
> Wash away all my iniquity,
> and cleanse me from my sin.
> For I know my transgressions,
> and my sin is always before me.
> Against you, you only, have I sinned

and done what is evil in your sight,
so that you are proved right when you speak
and justified when you judge.
Surely I was sinful at birth,
sinful from the time my mother conceive me.
Surely you desire truth in the inner parts;
you teach me wisdom in the inmost place.
Cleanse me with hyssop, and I will be clean;
wash me, and I will be whiter than snow.
Let me hear joy and gladness;
let the bones you have crushed rejoice.
Hide your face from my sins
and blot out all my iniquity.
Create in me a pure heart, O God,
and renew a steadfast spirit within me.
Do not cast me from your presence
or take your Holy Spirit from me.
Restore to me the joy of your salvation
and grant me a willing spirit, to sustain me.
Then I will teach transgressors your ways,
and sinners will turn back to you.
Save me from bloodguilt, O God,
the God who saves me,
and my tongue will sing of your righteousness.
O Lord, open my lips,
and my mouth will declare your praise.
You do not delight in sacrifice,
or I would bring it;
you do not take pleasure in burnt offerings.
The sacrifices of God are a broken spirit;
a broken and a contrite heart,
O God, you will not despise. (Psalm 51:1–17)

In my case, abortion was not an answer from God; it was my
answer and one suggested by a few others. Again, God does not

interfere with our free will. Consequences still have to run their course and often are for our benefit in the long run. Then again, that was not really what I had asked God for anyway.

God used my bad choice of having an abortion to bring me to Him; to catch my attention. I am now thankful for that.

I know the abortion was not by His design or direction, but He used what I did wrong. God is so great that He could use a mistake of mine, a perceived "great sin," to show His mercy and His love. He got to me where it hurt the most. He was right in there with me, hurting for me. I couldn't miss Him.

At first, I didn't want to accept God's love and mercy. I didn't think I deserved it in any amount. I stayed at that place a long time— too long, in fact.

This last choice, to follow Christ, was the place where I decided to turn around, though. It's the place where I changed from making bad choices to making good ones. The bad choices had gotten me to the place I where I was, and that was not altogether the best place to be.

The choice to turn in another direction came from my remorse for the bad choices I had made.

Let's follow that process for a bit.

REMORSE:

# ADMITTING CHOICE

I wonder how young women would answer if you asked them, "What does it feel like physically to be pregnant, especially early in pregnancy?" For the most part, I suspect they would answer, "No different than before."

It's easy for some men to be judgmental about women who choose abortions because men have no idea what women go through in pregnancy. Then again, we women don't have any idea either, until we go through it.

Early in my pregnancy, I felt no different than I ever had. The doctor informed me that I was pregnant, as I had missed my period. I had a small window of opportunity to make a huge decision about a "problem." The decision to abort the baby did not seem to be a big deal at the time. I knew that doctors performed abortions, and a doctor was going to assist in this procedure. I was seeing a solution to my problem through blinded and selfish eyes. This may sound crazy, but at this time in history clinics were not allowed to refer to your issue as anything more than a "problem"—*not* a baby.

At no point during my counseling at the clinic did they instruct me that I was actually ending the life of a human being, for they did not think I was.

I felt no remorse—yet.

Remorse begins as that first tiny inkling that you may have done something you shouldn't have. It may not even be conscious.

It develops into a conviction of wrongdoing, but it starts as just a passing thought.

Some people have no concept of wrongdoing, and they do not realize what they have done, other than having fixed a "problem" they had. Others choose to ignore the truth and the convictions and jump to fixing the problem. Where are you? Are you convicted? Have you ignored it? Have you wanted to change your mind?

Up to this point, there has been little or no repentance. Repentance is simply turning from one way of life, one path, to another. It is used in reference to turning from a worldly path to the path God would like us to follow.

I can't say that I understood fully what I had done until I carried my firstborn to term. It was at that point that I began to agonize over what I had done. Even during this second pregnancy, I did not understand. I had to hold the child before I could go back to my abortion in my mind and realize that I had terminated a human life. I felt stupid about this. I still do some days.

When people talk about abortion, in general, they may envision a fully developed baby. But for the most part, abortions are carried out before the mother has signs of pregnancy—no weight gain, illness, or movement sensations. There is no indication of another life inside her.

I believe that some of us women do not think of the pregnancy as a full baby growing inside, although others who look at us do. This leaves us at a disadvantage of not fully realizing what is going on. Only after the baby is born do we understand.

The overwhelming remorse I felt through the years, following the birth of my firstborn, caused me great pain in my heart and throughout my entire body. The anguish and remorse was unbearable at times. God has since released me from many of those feelings, and I'm very grateful. I still have the occasional regretful pain, which *I* bring up, not God.

At some point after having an abortion, I'm sure that most women realize that the fetus was most certainly a child, a human being, created by God. And many know full well that the blood of that child is on their hands, and they look for relief, which is where we're hoping to go.

Guilt can be our worst enemy or a friend that brings remorse. The guilt we feel can either drive us deeper into the ground of self-condemnation or direct us through remorse toward restoration with God.

At some point in my life, I had a desire to stand in front of the church and give them stones so they could stone me to death—that's how awful I felt. I wanted to shout it on top of the mountain so the whole world would know that I was guilty, and maybe somehow, that would relieve me of some of my pain—or at least punish me appropriately.

There are days when I wish I could sit with this unborn child and caress their hair, have a long talk, and embrace them, as I have with my living children. I even have a mental picture of the gender, hair, appearance, and so on, of this child. She has grown up despite me, in a sense. She may not be present with me in this life, but I know we will be together in the next. I even asked her, in my heart, to forgive me for my decision. I sense her forgiveness, similar to that of Christ. Because Christ has forgiven me, she has also.

Please note that we do not believe this child is dead. The prevenient, or preceding, grace of God provides for the redemption of these young ones during the period before reaching the age of accountability. God takes care of them at the level where they are, not the level where we are.

I would not have sought forgiveness had it not been for remorse. The remorse, or deep regret, brought me to the place where I felt the need for forgiveness. It's part of the healing process.

With this kind of severe issue in life, we often repeat in our minds the same emotions, over and over again, never choosing to deal with or face them head-on. We get stuck. The pain is so intense sometimes that we feel trapped and believe we can't move on from those feelings of shame and guilt. Finding true freedom seems impossible from the prison we've created in our minds, in order to protect and punish ourselves.

Sounds strange, perhaps, but it is protecting ourselves from others finding out the truth and punishing ourselves by living in secret, both at the same time.

*This kind of life is not necessary!*

I could go through all the details of how an abortion is conducted, but if you want that information, search the internet. It all comes down to the same result: the end of a human life. We have to go through a mourning process, with God's divine help and touch. We can live productive and joyful lives, blessed by God, with abundant life and soaring on eagle's wings (Isaiah 40:31).

Believe me; it is possible with Jesus on our side. A caution: looking at yourself can create a tremendous amount of pain. Be prepared for that. The walk on which you are about to embark is one well worth taking.

It has become the most amazing love-walk I have ever encountered. It is my walk with my best friend, Redeemer, Savior, Prince of Peace, comforter, wonderful counselor, and Lord of my life.

He is on my side, and He is on your side.

With me, the remorse became so deep-seated that there were times when I would seem to have an out-of-body experience; I would look at myself in the mirror and say things like, "How could you do that?" or "How could you be so stupid?" Now, I can't understand how I allowed myself to do such a thing as abortion. My choice would be totally against abortion now. There are times when we are our own worst accuser and I was.

When I got pregnant, I could not put my life aside for the life of the child, so I chose to end the life of the child. (Even when we feel like moral failures, we have an overpowering will to survive. This will to survive usually only wins at the expense of others.)

Christ's statement in John 15:13—"Greater love has no one than this, that he lay down his life for his friends"—can apply here. Can we love a child, even an unborn one, so much that we will lay aside our lives to raise that child?

Yes, we can, but it doesn't happen until we choose it. We do not start out loving like that. Children—and we all start out as children in every aspect of life—must learn everything, including love.

When I began this book, all I could see were fields of women who'd had abortions and all the little babies waiting in heaven. I neglected the fields of men who also played a part in this scenario. Some might not even realize they had a part in someone's aborting a child; others might be the reason why a woman chose that path. At some point, they must acknowledge, before God, their sin, for they will be held accountable. They too must ask forgiveness.

I see fields of souls waiting for the harvest. Satan uses self-righteousness to battle God for souls, sometimes because they don't accept what is freely theirs to take—forgiveness. It appears as though abortion is strictly women's sin, but they were not alone—although they often were left standing alone. The men are a harvest field all on their own.

We shared with others when we got into the mess; what makes us think we should not share with them in the solution?

If any man who has had a sexual encounter, within or outside of marriage, is not sure of the outcome, he may have a hand in an abortion without knowing it. Does that make you think, men? It should! Think carefully about what you are responsible for. You may find remorse in your life for your participation.

Some young women or girls may have been forced by their parents to abort a child against their wills. Those parents too are responsible. They too may experience remorse.

But we can't look back with accusing fingers against anyone. We defeat the purpose if we go back with the intention of blaming someone else, whether it's our parents or the man involved. Ultimately, the only reason for going back in an attempt to deal with this issue is to come before God for forgiveness for our parts. As individuals, we are only responsible for ourselves before God. God will deal with the others in His own way.

We cannot force our beliefs or repentance on anyone else. I am thankful that God has allowed me not to harbor any wrong feelings toward the father of the unborn child. If we do, then we have to come to the place where we can forgive him also. This may even have to happen before we can forgive ourselves. Do you ever blame the father? How about your parents? Or do you blame only yourself?

To forgive myself was the hardest thing to do. It is easy for any of us to just choose to stay where we are in our walk with God. We find it too painful to think of what we allowed ourselves to do, and we feel so foolish and disgusted with ourselves.

My disrespect for myself was so overwhelming that I felt God could not look at me, let alone love me. The love I had for myself was slowly but steadily being chipped away. I specifically remember reading in my Bible, *"Rejoice in the Lord always. I will say it again: Rejoice!"* (Philippians 4:4) and singing about joy with little children in Sunday school, yet I wondered why I did not and could not have any joy within myself. I had been robbed completely of any happy thoughts, and I had no hope—or so I thought.

I decided then that I did not want to live that way any more. I sought the Lord in earnest.

Even the blame game is a form of remorse.

Before remorse, there is no repentance from the actions taken. Remorse is the first tiny step of repentance. It is the step that says, "I may have done something wrong."

Repentance is a turn from one way of life or thinking to another. In this case, it is the turn from thinking abortion is OK to thinking it is wrong. It is the first time we recognize a viewpoint other than the one we see with our own eyes.

Our eyes see what we want but not what others may want. Remorse admits there are other things to see. Repentance allows other viewpoints to be introduced, even God's. This can be painful, but we need to acknowledge that this is only part of the repentance process. Seeing the truth about what we did is admitting that the viewpoint of some others may be valid, and we may be wrong. This part of the process can take time, and we may need to allow ourselves that time. Just don't forget to move on eventually.

Again, there are different views on when a fetus becomes a person—the moment of individual creation. My view is that it all life begins at conception.

I did not always have this opinion. When I felt remorse, I began to repent and turn from my old opinion to this new one.

Remorse can play tricks with you as well. Opening yourself up to anyone about your part is a risky business. You could face extreme disappointment from your spouse, parents, children, friends, or anyone, but the remorse drives you to admission of involvement. You are compelled to tell your story.

I encourage you to be careful in this. Do not tell just anyone. Many will not be sympathetic or empathetic. They can easily be rude and blunt and drive you into a deeper hole. Pick your confidants well, and keep them few.

What Alma is talking about in this chapter is the beginning of the hope I indicated is possible for all who keep on trying. The remorse she is talking about is the first sign that you want to change. Change is what repentance is. Repentance is the change from one way of life or way of being to another way of life or way of being. Repenting is turning from the way you are going to the other way.

True repentance is turning from anything in us, about us, or from us to everything God.

Some people turn from sin to righteousness immediately; there is no lag time. Others struggle with the turn, and the process takes some time. Neither should discard or discredit the other. Either way, turning to God is right, whether the turn is instantaneous or a process.

Remorse indicates you do not want to be the way you are anymore. You want to change. This is the first step of repentance. I call this *initial repentance*. If this is followed through to its end, a full repentance is possible, and the fullness of repentance is attainable.

Following is a chart on the process of repentance. The chart may become clearer for you as you see yourself turn. The little arrows point toward the direction in which you are heading. The highlighted one is what this part speaks of. It is the first turn slightly away from sin. Perhaps you are at some stage in the middle. The end is in sight for each of us. There is hope in the Lord. Trust and believe.

> That if you confess with your mouth, "Jesus is Lord,"
> and believe in your heart that God hath raised him
> from the dead, you will be saved. (Romans 10:9)

There was no need to show the chart before this because it would have meant very little. Now, there is some progress to show on the chart. That is encouraging.

You'll see this chart a few more times as we discuss this subject. Each time, there will be a little more explanation and a little more progress. Strive for the end result.

| The Process of Repentance | | | | |
|---|---|---|---|---|
| Sin | Remorse | Repentance | Working Repentance | Righteousness |
| our will | | | | God's will |
| absence of repentance | initial repentance | recognition of repentance | repentance at work | fullness of repentance |
| ← | \ | ↑ | / | → |
| Direction of focus | | | | |

## GUILTY AS CHARGED:

# ACCEPTING CHOICE

"Who did such a thing? Was it me? I didn't know I could be so evil."

When I permit myself to look back and imagine what that baby went through during the abortion, I can't help but be very disgusted with myself. I believe the baby did not realize what was happening, but there was still a form of suffering.

Now, I can rest on the fact that Jesus was there, even when I did not recognize Him, even when I didn't know what I was doing. He was there, ready to welcome my baby into His kingdom. The angels were all around; they were encamped around us both. I am most certain I was grieving God, but He still loved me, even at that moment. He was ready to forgive me at that time too. All I had to do was ask and turn to Him.

Having sinned against God, He patiently waited until I realized my need to turn to Him for forgiveness. My biggest need at the time was realizing I was guilty. I was keeping it a secret from myself as much as anyone. During this time, He gently called me to Him.

If you cringe inside every time the word *abortion* is mentioned, or you cannot say the word aloud, you are still in the process. There's often a felt need to talk about it with others to see if they will still accept you. At the same time, the feelings of validity cannot be undermined with half truths from others, such as, "Oh, it's not that bad." We need total acceptance and acknowledgment of what we have done and of ourselves.

Without validation, many turn to silence and secrecy.

Let's talk about secrecy for a moment.

Keeping our secrets often leads to hiding more secrets. When we decide we can let our big secret go, we can let all secrecy go. Nothing is then secret anymore, at least with some people. A healthy balance should be struck somewhere between too much and too little.

Secrecy is often accompanied by fear. It is the fear of being found out; the fear that someone else will know what was done and who did it. This is probably attached to a fear of rejection by others, in the case of a personal secret.

Like Adam and Eve, we even want to hide from God what we have done. We want to hide the mistakes, the sins we commit, because deep down, no matter what we may say with our mouths, we know we have done wrong.

Our mouths may say we think that abortion is acceptable, but we still may hide in shame. Our mouths may say the law allows certain things, and we will uphold the law, but our hearts still grieve and mourn. Our mouths may say we do not believe in God or a higher life force, but if we did not, there would be no reason for rules at all—no order, only chaos in our lives. The fact that we submit to rules and order demonstrates our underlying belief in a higher authority. We believe that is God.

Christianity teaches us that there is a higher authority than human judgment can understand. We know that higher authority— namely, God— overrules our laws or our human ethics. Ultimately, we all know this, but we may not be willing to admit to it or submit to it.

I personally managed to keep my abortion a secret for many years from many people. I had the control of who I would allow to know. I could have chosen to keep it a secret for a lifetime if I wanted to, but I could not keep it a secret from God, even for a minute. He has always known my secret, even before it existed.

There are many places where abortion is legal. That does not make it right to do. We know that and still try to hide behind the human legalization, rather than face the divine decree, the real truth, God's truth.

This is a private matter. It is only by the grace of God and His calling that Alma wishes to tell her story. For most, this and other issues that are private will remain as such. They will not remain secret from God, however, only private, and that is OK. Though God knows all about each mistake and sin, we hide it from Him—or so we think. The "secrecy" from God will be broken when we admit to Him that we have sinned. Then, the lifeline of a relationship with Him will be reattached; a relationship will be renewed.

Many women who have abortions have never had children before. They only realize exactly what they have done when they are blessed with other children. I was that way.

I was so weighed down by my sin and bondage that my feet were heavy. I would do great things for God, trying to measure up. I would push myself to do things I didn't want to do—church things, neighbor things—*never* finding any more freedom or worthiness.

I would frequently judge others, knowing full well I was no better than they, but I could not get my eyes off them. I could not say no to anything good asked of me. I felt God was always watching my every move. I would try to work my way through to God, but that did not work either.

It could be a beautiful day outside—the sun shining and the birds singing—and I'd feel overwhelmed and gloomy. I and others climb out of bed, and the first thing we face is the mirror. We either avoid looking in it, or we do not truly see ourselves.

Do not merely listen to the word and so deceive yourselves. Do what it says. Anyone who listens to the word but does not do what it says, is like a man who looks at his face in a mirror and, after looking at himself, goes away and immediately forgets what he looks like. But the man who looks intently into the perfect law that gives freedom, and continues to do this, not forgetting what he has heard, but doing it –he will be blessed in what he does. (James 1:22–25)

What can I say, but I love You, Lord and thank you?

God's holiness is so pure that He cannot look upon me without my being covered by the blood of Christ. But God could not look upon me even before I had my abortion. I had to repent of *all* my sin and accept Christ as my Savior. I had to admit I was a sinner, even without the abortion. We all have to admit we are guilty sinners to a holy God in order to be acceptable. We all have to be covered by the blood of Jesus.

Jesus was and is the Son of God. He came to be the sacrifice that would pay for our sin. The sacrifice had to be the blood of a perfect firstborn. That would have been an animal in older times.

But when Jesus came, He was the only perfect sacrifice that ever was available. Jesus was crucified—nailed to a cross as an innocent man. He was completely innocent of any sin in His life. That innocence perfectly atoned (made full payment) for sin, where all the previous animal sacrifices had fallen short.

It is only the blood of Christ Jesus that can truly atone for our sin. That blood is available to all who will repent of sin, ask God for forgiveness, and turn to Jesus as Savior. That is what being covered by the blood of Jesus is all about.

I often wonder exactly what I was thinking then, and I am left confused by it. I no longer think that way, but it took time for me to change. In that time, I repented. Then, I allowed it to fully penetrate my being.

Beautiful women are often gripped in fear if they truly look into the mirror. If they look too closely, they fear they will look at their sin and shame and maybe even catch God watching.

I say *beautiful women* because we are all beautiful in our own way. And we are all beautiful to God.

We all look intently in the mirror in search of telltale signs of our guilt that the world might see. We search, dreading the inevitable exposure. Whether the world sees or not, we see it clearly.

We know the secret we are trying to hide from the world,

ourselves, and God. The longer we hide, the more we hate ourselves. But there is freedom in Christ.

John 8:32 says, "The truth will set you free." The truth is, we don't deserve forgiveness. What we did was murder. But God did not tell the sinners, "Oh, your sin is so much greater than the other guy's." He didn't tell the prostitute, "Your sin is worse than Zacchaeus, the tax collector." He did not make any sin worse than another, nor did He make any sin better than another. They were all sinners. We are all sinners. God does not measure sin.

God will be the first to tell us that we are guilty of sin, and we must accept it, but in His mercy, He can forgive.

> For all have sinned, and fall short of the glory of God, and are justified freely by his grace through the redemption that came by Christ Jesus. (Romans 3:23–24)

> For the wages of sin is death, but the gift of God is eternal life in Christ Jesus our Lord. (Romans 6:23)

Unfortunately, God usually has to wait for us to get out of our own way. We know we are guilty as charged—and we want to punish ourselves for it.

## SELF-CONDEMNATION:

# JUDGING CHOICE

We feel self-condemnation, self-destruction, and self-affliction with the help of Satan and his lies. Satan is a master of lies, and he is very good at getting us to believe the worst. Sometimes, with the help of others, we find ourselves with repetitive, negative thoughts. We afflict ourselves with the most degrading ones.

Easy to do, hard to explain. It is very easy for us to condemn ourselves; it is difficult to explain why or how we do it.

Whoever gave us the idea that we would make good judges? Wherever it came from, most of us have the notion that our opinions are more important than anyone else's.

That's what self-condemnation is—judging ourselves, passing an opinion on ourselves. We may consider it as final, superseding all other judgments on the case, and irreversible. There are times when we may consider our judgment over God's. He can say we're forgiven, yet we don't forgive ourselves. This leaves us wondering why we have the right to override God's judgment.

We do the same thing to each other, as though we know better than the other.

Some of the comments I have heard over the years have included:
"Does your husband know?"
"Abortion is murder."
"That's the worst thing a person could do!"
I thought I must be feeling somewhat like Christ felt when He was dying on the cross. "My God, my God, why have you forsaken

me?" God did not forsake Jesus, but these people seemed to have forsaken me.

Some declared me to be the biggest sinner alive. I didn't need their help to do that; I was already doing it to myself. I was already condemning myself for my sin.

Jesus promises that He will not forsake us, even in our stupid mistakes. We are loved, with or without the errors we make.

My question is, does anybody truly believe in the power of the cross for forgiveness?

I cannot imagine how much I have disappointed God in my sinning against Him. I found it hard to let go of what a great sin I had committed. I thought God could surely never forgive me for it. I stayed in those thoughts for a long time. It was overwhelming, at times, to think of what I had done.

And then, years roll by when we try desperately hard to suppress what we have done. We try not to think about it or talk about it. We definitely do not share our secret with just anyone. Occasionally, we dare to share it with a select few—people we hope will love us anyhow. That's the way we may cope with our secret (at least, I did).

We listen to others and what their views are on the subject, even though we try to avoid the subject, if at all possible. Listening to others often only reinforces our conviction of guilt and shame. We never express an opinion—oh, maybe an occasional *uh-huh*. Then the cycle starts all over again—"Just don't think about it; take those opinions and put them with the rest"—in the depths of our souls to torment us even more.

The thoughts do go to the backs of our minds, but they don't stay there, even if we think they do. The waters are still disturbed just below the surface. We have to begin the process of transferring our guilt onto our Lord Jesus Christ.

In our subconscious minds, we can deal with issues our conscious minds are incapable of handling. Although we may not trust ourselves, much can be accomplished this way.

If we can fool the world to think we are innocent and that

everything is OK, maybe we can fool ourselves into thinking the same, and we won't have to face it. Meanwhile, Satan has fooled all of us into staying in our cages with the doors wide open. We stay in the cage because of our fear. Jesus is the door.

> Jesus answered, "I am the way and the truth and the life. No one comes to the Father except through me." (John 14:6)

> Ask and it will be given you; seek and you will find; knock and the door will be opened to you. For everyone that asks receives; he who seeks finds; and to him who knocks, the door will be opened.
> Which of you, if his son asks for bread, will give him a stone? Or if he asks for a fish, will give him a snake? If you, then, though you are evil [a sinner], know how to give good gifts to your children, how much more will your Father in heaven give good gifts to those who ask him! So in everything do to others what you would have them do to you, for this sums up the Law and the Prophets. (Matthew 7:7–12)

Talk about disappointment—God also could be frustrated and exasperated that *we do not take His Word as truth* and that His grace *is* sufficient. That may be a great disappointment to God because we are saying that Jesus died for nothing. We are demeaning everything about Jesus's death on the cross. We are refusing Jesus's free gift of the cross. But it is for us. We may not understand, but God continues to love us through our rebellion, as well as in good times.

I realized how disappointed God could have been during all those years that He waited for me to recognize that His grace was sufficient to cover my abortion and so many other issues.

Before you go on a self-condemning slide into oblivion, look at a few soul-searching questions.

On the premise that a question asked always requires an answer, sooner or later, here are some questions for you to ponder:

1. Do you know the dictionary meanings of faith, trust, grace, mercy, love, and forgiveness?

    I knew what these words meant, but reading the dictionary definitions elaborated on them. God touched me through them when I opened myself up to Him and His definition.

2. As a child, how did you view sin? Was your church an influence in this view?

    My church impressed upon me, as a child, that different sins had different outcomes with God.

3. Did your parents' view of abortion affect your decision?

    The fear of disappointing my parents overruled any reasoning, good or bad.

4. What had the most or any influence on the decision you made?

    Some of the most influential things for me have only come to light in my old age.

5. Did the clinic or doctor claim the truth about what you were doing—causing death?

6. Were you able to find a friend you could trust, one who could acknowledge what you did?

    Randy was, by far, the most understanding, loving, and accepting, but I also needed outside help. A few close friends filled in as well.

7. What form of abortion did you have?

8. Has this event come back to haunt you?

9.  What caused that haunting to erupt?

10. Do you have feelings of unworthiness, wondering why God has chosen to bless you again?

    It always amazes me that God still chose to bless me with two absolutely wonderful children after my abortion.

11. Do you feel the need to share with others?

12. Do you expect that others can punish you for the guilt or set you free?

13. Spiritual guilt is not an earthly problem, so why look for an earthly solution?

    Seeking acceptance from people is commendable, but God is the only true healer.

14. Do you view one sin as worse than another? Do you think this is so in God's eyes?

15. Are you under conviction by the Holy Spirit?

16. Do the views of an emotional female and a logical male differ?

    People deal with issues differently. Randy can see things as black or white, while I have a lot of gray areas I add for the sake of my emotions.

17. How deep is God's forgiveness and love for you?
    (Check out John 3:16; 15:13; Psalm 103:12)

18. There are as many men involved as there are women, so where are they?

    We women often are left holding the bag, but God still knows about men's involvement.

19. Should you talk with parents, friends, or siblings?
    Only you can decide.

20. Do the churches you have attended preach grace when talking about issues like this?
    Rarely do we find unconditional grace in our churches, but God is still God, and God's grace is sufficient.

21. Can you say the word *abortion*? If not, there is a problem.
    It was hard for me to say the word *abortion* for many years. If I didn't say it, I found it easier to disconnect from it.

I have found freedom in Christ, but there is always a level of fear and tension that goes with it. As I wrote this book, I could sense that my whole body was full of anxiety at times.

We do not want people to know we are reading material on abortions, for fear of being found out. But Jesus says in Matthew 10:26, "So do not be afraid of them. There is nothing concealed that will not be disclosed, or hidden that will not be known." That's where the freedom lies. As long as we hide, we will never find freedom in Christ. Nothing is hidden from Him anyway.

The weight of guilt about my abortion became overwhelming to me. There appeared to be no place to turn for relief. I was regularly attending church and actively teaching Sunday school. All the while, however, my mind was full of accusations toward myself.

Our pastor had a sermon series on how abortions were wrong. My guilt rose even more. I sobbed—this was a regular occurrence for a few Sundays. Although it was many years ago, I clearly remember sitting at the back of the church, crying my heart out. I had accepted Christ as my Savior years before, but I had never given my abortion over to Him.

We left the church that morning, and I was broken. As we walked out of the church, it was just beginning to snow—I had the song "Whiter than Snow" in my head because we'd sung it that morning. Our drive home was only ten minutes, but by the time we got there, it was a blizzard. We both saw each snowflake as one sin that God forgave. God used that snowy morning to speak to me and show me that He can make the snow as deep as necessary to cover all our sins. If it takes a blizzard, He can provide one for His children.

Later that day, as I was still mourning, Randy asked me if I had truly asked God for forgiveness. I knew I had, but I had no assurance that He would want to forgive me.

Through my tears, my son came up and wanted to talk to me. Randy tried to send him away since I was such a mess. I said, "No, let him come to me." As I listened to my son, I asked myself what could he be guilty of that I, as his mother, would turn away from him. What would take away the fact that I was his mother?

Nothing! Simply nothing. I love him, and he is my son.

I heard God say to me, "Alma, you are My child, and nothing you do can take you away from Me. I love you, and you are My daughter." I *believed* it, and my healing truly began.

God used my relationship with my son to show me who I was to Him in a very powerful way.

I was trying very hard to hide my sin from the world, but after a while, I realized that God knew all about it. I could not hide from Him. God was the one I should be concerned with and God was the only one who could help me.

Of course, all those suppressed emotions, guilt, and shame wreak havoc on our bodies. Health problems may arise, such as depression. We don't like ourselves very much or who we have become, never mind loving ourselves. There is a conflict here because we are not bad people, *but* we feel like we are. How could a just God look at us, let alone forgive us or love us?

That is our justice talking, not God's.

Then we get on the journey of trying to work our way out of the hole we have dug, the mess we have created, the foolish mistake we have made. "How stupid can I be?" I tormented myself with that question for many, many years.

People may reinforce those thoughts of stupidity, in the world and in the church. It's a strange setup because the world says it's acceptable—but not really. The church says it's forgivable—but not really. So where do we stand? *In front of Christ!*

Abortion is not the worst thing a person can do. Not accepting Christ as Savior, not discovering forgiveness, not finding freedom in Jesus, not becoming on fire (*hot, hot, hot*) for God is the worst thing.

Our education clouds our vision of who God is because we end up trusting more in ourselves than in Him. Trusting ourselves and our choices is not always the wisest choice. I struggle with trust issues still today, both trusting myself and others.

We live in a time when people seem to be more educated than they were seventy-five years ago. I view this as a distraction because we can become more reliant on our own understanding than on God's supernatural power. We live in the I-can-do-it-myself generation, but this forgiveness thing—we cannot do that ourselves.

Not dealing with the hard struggles and wrong choices in life can be like lying down in a coffin while we are still alive. The lid may be wide open to the coffin, but the coffin is made up of Satan's lies, and we choose to lay in it. We believe Satan's lies of "My sin is too great for God to forgive," or "You don't understand; I've done so many wrong things."

But, my friend, our not believing that God's grace *is* sufficient, that God's truth *does* set us free, and that God's love *is* great enough allows Satan a foothold in our minds, hearts, and souls. What a tool for Satan to use against the women of today. For years, our churches were filled with God-fearing women working for God. Today, we lose more and more of these women because they haven't come to the place in their lives where they see or acknowledge that God has truly touched them with His grace. How sad!

## LET IT GET WORSE:

# CHOICE CHANGERS

In our lives, we might pray, "Lord, if need be, let my circumstances be worsened, should that bring me closer to You."

Getting worse is not necessarily a bad thing. Surgeons may tell you that a growth needs to get bigger in order to warrant an operation. Mechanics may tell you a certain ominous sound needs to get worse or change to something else before repairs are in order. Many things must get to a critical point before changes are called for. So if our intent is truly to glorify God, then there is sense in sometimes praying, "Lord, let things get worse, if it will help."

I still remember the first time I heard "let things get worse"—how peculiar it sounded. It was so much against my way of thinking and against my way of life. It was like praying badness on someone. I had been raised in a society that taught that things should always be easy. If I was blessed with material possessions and if things were going well and I was getting my way, then I must be in God's will. It was the old health-and-wealth mentality—you are only healthy and wealthy if you are being good.

To start praying for someone we love—praying for things to get worse—requires a higher level of faith in God and His wisdom. To place full trust in God and His ways or to relinquish our meager control over any factors in another person's life certainly stirs some fear in us. We are human, after all. It draws from us a level of trust that our almighty God is looking out for our ultimate best. So what is our ultimate best in God's view? It is that we actually become believers and are truly saved by God's grace. Our ultimate best is to be His children.

But to pray things actually get worse? What a thought.

I learned very little that was useful to God when things were going well and going my way—what I thought was best. That typically is the less painful life; at least, I believed it was the less painful life. I ended up learning more in tough times and through hard lessons.

Where did God fit in all this back then? I don't think He was taking up too much of my time, my thoughts, or my life before I became pregnant. It amazes me that even when I had no thought of God, He did not forget me.

God was still waiting for me. He wanted to draw me nearer to Him. Strangely, when I first found out I was pregnant, my thoughts turned to God. Go figure. I recognized God's power in my pregnancy, but I wonder if I also blamed Him initially.

For someone who had given no thought or mind to God on a regular basis, I quickly looked to God for help and answers—conditionally, of course, for I had my own predetermined solutions: miscarry the baby, or …

Our society seems geared to believe that we are in control of our destinies and of things going on around us. But we actually control a very minute number of the circumstances in our world. Much of our lives are dependent on the decisions others make. Realizing this can help us understand the concept of allowing the situations of life to get worse. It can help us get to the point where we can pray that they do get worse so that we can get past them to better things.

I had to allow things to get pretty bad.

I remember the day I said to God, "I have messed up my life so bad"—thinking about my abortion and other things—"that surely *You* can do better, so You can have it." My wrong choice to have an abortion brought me to the place, eventually, of the *best* choice of my entire life; I chose Jesus as my Savior.

God granted me free will and allowed me to control my own destiny. In other words, I could choose which way I wanted to live, now and eternally. This freedom allowed me to see who He is, as it can with each of us. God was always there for me to see, but I still needed to look. Some people don't want to believe what they see. For a long time, I was one of them.

Without having made the mistake I did, I might not have come to know God. He worked through my mistake to bring me to a knowledge of Him. I'm so thankful I came to the end of myself and turned to God for healing.

Before choosing to follow Christ as my Savior, I had to get to the end of myself. I just seemed to be digging my hole deeper and deeper. Some use the analogy of getting to the bottom of the barrel, but it is simply coming to the end of ourselves in some way.

Thankfully I got to the end of myself in order to find Him. All the way to the end.

Have you gotten to that point in your life yet? Have you begun to choose differently than you did? Have you come to the end of yourself—your former self?

Sometimes we are there and just don't recognize it.

As you can see, this is one of those ways God helps to change your choices. Alma was brought to a new understanding of life and the consequences of her choices. Now, she makes different choices than she did before.

That steps into repentance.

## INTERVENTION:

# WHO'S BUGGING ME?

There's a story about a man caught in a flood. As the water advances on his house, a boat comes by to rescue him. He tells the boatmen that he will trust his God to save him. A second boat comes by as the water reaches the eaves, and he is on the roof of the house. His response is the same for this rescue attempt; he will wait for God.

As the man holds tight to the chimney, the water laps at his ankles and a helicopter arrives—his last chance for a rescue. Again, he says he will wait for God. The helicopter flies off to rescue someone willing to be rescued.

In the end, the man dies and ends up in the judgment room. He asks why God did not come to rescue him. The answer God gives is this: "I sent you two boats and a helicopter. What more did you want?"

This funny little story makes a very good point that we need to address: *don't miss the opportunities given to you.*

This begs the question, "What opportunities?" God gives us each an entire lifetime of opportunities to come to Him for rescue. We can't afford to miss them. These opportunities are God's intervention to rescue us.

God comes to visit each of us, once in a while. The Holy Spirit of God intervenes in our lives by sending messages. Books, friends, pastors, a class, a tugging at the heart—there are many ways the Lord sends us messages to help us along.

Some people call these messages their conscience; some people refer to it as "that little voice in my head"; I think the messages are from the Holy Spirit of God. What is the message? It is that nagging inside that tells us we should be doing something or not doing something. It is that phenomenon of intelligence that leads us to review and reevaluate any given situation, to check our first reaction. It is God telling us what He would like us to do.

I firmly believe that we are incapable of thinking these messages on our own; therefore, God helps us out. Why do I say this? Because our first, selfish reaction is what we would do if left unchecked. We have no reason to review or reevaluate our actions. If left to ourselves, we would always do as we please, not as we should.

So how does God accomplish this? God gave us an understanding of the difference between right and wrong. We have that understanding inherent within us. We know our first reaction is selfish, but then we see a way of not being selfish. Sometimes this is through our own consideration, and sometimes it is derived from the influence of others. If it's stirred within us, then it must be from another source. I believe this source is God. If it is through others, then it has stirred in them, and again, I believe the source of that stirring is God. Remember that God told us from the beginning what is right and what is wrong. We have no valid excuses.

In any case, it ends up coming to us through books, conversations, songs, or any other means of communications. It even seems to come as a movement in the heart or a change in attitude or outlook. However it comes, God communicates His message to us in some way so we know what we should do. He intervenes in our lives on our behalf to draw us closer to Him.

God wants to rescue us. That's what being saved is—rescue from danger. But He always grants us the freedom to choose to accept or refuse His rescue.

Which should you choose today? Which *will* you choose today?

In order to be comfortable looking in the mirror, we need to be transparent.

Consider the word *transparent*; it is applied to something we can see through, like glass. With regard to people, it means that their feelings are apparent, or their attitudes or personalities are obvious.

Transparent is being able and willing to view the inner person along with the outward person.

Transparency shows us and others how we view ourselves. It is the key to acceptance with your spouse or others and with God. Transparency shows just who we are to our friends, spouse, world, church, and God.

We are not transparent in all situations. We may venture only so far in showing some of the major issues of life, and then we become stuck because we feel it's too risky to take another chance. Why are we stuck? Often, this is because we desperately need total acceptance, unconditional love, and trust, but we don't expect it.

There's a small lesson for us. Being transparent to God includes being known by Him when no one else can see. God accepts us, no matter what. Perhaps we should accept each other, no matter what, as well. *No matter what* could be a good battle cry for those who would love as Christ loves us.

Strangely enough, as much as I attempted to hide my secret from myself, others, and God, I could not fool God. He already knew the truth, and I could not hide from Him. I am transparent to Him—not by choice; I just am.

Even when we try to hide from God, He still intervenes on our behalf. He still allowed His Son, Jesus, to die for us. No matter how much God can see of us, He still loves us.

The apostle Paul tells us about God's love for us:

> For I am convinced that neither death nor life,
> neither angels nor demons, neither the present nor
> the future, nor any powers, neither height nor depth,
> nor anything else in all creation, will be able to

separate us from the love of God, that is in Christ
Jesus our Lord. (Romans 8:38–39)

I was somewhat like Adam and Eve, hiding in the garden after
eating the fruit from the forbidden tree. They attempted to hide from
God, but God already knew what they had done and that they were
trying to hide from Him. God can see through us; we are transparent
to Him, no matter what.

Some have said of my abortion, "Oh, it's not that bad." I feel
that unless they are willing to admit fully the scope of my abortion,
they are not fully accepting me. I explain this to them, and they
usually realize how significant this is in my life. Finally, my full
transparency with them and their full acceptance of me leaves a clear
impression on me that I am loved just as I am. Without being allowed
transparency, I might not have felt fully loved. Therefore, by living
in secret, we may never fully feel acceptable to anyone.

Here are two reasons for desperately feeling like yelling on
a rooftop and wanting acceptance from others: (1) a desire to tell
others the truth; to own up, and (2) a felt need for people to love us
and accept us for who we are, with our faults.

The comment, "That's the worst thing anyone could do," leaves
you never feeling like you could reach the mark—their mark, that
perfect mark. How can you become perfect in the sight of God with
a past like this? Unfortunately, some of our churches have the worst-
thing-you-could-do philosophy. But God reacts with His love and
grace instead.

"For my thoughts are not your thoughts, neither are
your ways my ways," declares the LORD. (Isaiah
55:8)

Can you imagine for one minute that God does not view us as
people do? God is much more forgiving, and we are transparent to
Him. I am thankful He did not approach me with the worst-thing-
you-could-do attitude. Instead, He left me to my own thoughts and

loved me anyway. God has known my comings and goings and has chosen to walk beside me all the way.

Throughout my life, I have returned to Isaiah 55:8 many times. It reminds me to check whether I am dealing with the human way of looking at things or God's way. Who's bugging me? God is! That's what intervention is.

I often have encountered people who are judgmental and unforgiving. God is not that way. It's well worth it for us to be bugged by God's love and grace.

I felt like people could see through me. I wanted desperately to hide. If God knows my thoughts, He knows all, people don't.

God has a way of weaving through our minds and lives and leaving His footprints along the way.

One afternoon, over tea, I entered into a serious discussion with a friend, and I told about my abortion. For some unknown reason, out of my mouth came a bit about my being sexually assaulted. What an opening. God just made a clear way for others to share their stories. Unconditional acceptance of them equaled unconditional acceptance of me. God worked through that encounter and others.

There is a certain level of freedom in becoming totally transparent with our friends, spouse, family, and God. Most times, we need to deal with God first to become comfortable with being transparent because we usually need forgiveness before we can have freedom enough to be fully transparent.

If He is for you, who can be against you?

> What, then, shall we say in response to this? If God is for us, who can be against us? (Romans 8:31)

We live our lives, thinking God is against us, but we need to move to the other side of life, where there is true life and living water, and realize that He is for us, and we need no other to sustain us.

We should be comfortable and yearning to come to the foot of God's throne. There is a turning around not only in becoming a new creature in Christ but also in becoming at peace at His throne. There is no place so peaceful. "If God is for us, who can be against us?"

God intervenes in our lives, each of them, in the way only He can. He urges us to come to Him, to ask His forgiveness, and to turn our lives around to Him.

Just as we may intervene in the lives of our loved ones to turn them from a dangerous path, God intervenes in our lives because He loves us. He loves us so much that He sent His Son to redeem us.

I'm glad God is one who does not give up easily. I'm glad He hangs around, not only to nag us but also to help us to transfer our sin from our selfish hands to Christ so that we can become a new creation in this same Jesus.

# Transition 2

## Basic Repentance:
### The Choice to Transit to Salvation

True, honest repentance is what God requires from us. It includes a long, hard look at ourselves and facing the facts—the truth about to what our choices have led us. It is more than facing God with our mess and acknowledging what we have done. It's turning away from that life and to God. Unless we get to this particular point at some time, God won't help us, at least not eternally. He may be nearby, drawing us toward Him, but it's our choice either to go away or to turn toward Him.

We may choose (again, a choice) to go through with repentance or turn back because of fear of what God will see in us or do to us. Remember, Satan, the deceiver, doesn't give up easily so his lies will resound in our ears. He'll tell us that it's too great a sin for God to forgive and that we were stupid, then and now, so why would this be any better choice than it was back then? Satan does not give up easily, so be prepared for his attack. We can write down some of the things going through our minds and check them out to see if they align with God's Word. If they don't, then we can discard them.

God is in the business of setting us free. The Bible says so:

> Then you will know the truth, and the truth will set you free. (John 8:32)

> So if the Son sets you free, you will be free indeed. (John 3:36)

Again, God is calling us to be transparent before Him.

Repentance is turning from any practice we believe offends God and turning to the practices that please Him. This requires that we change our minds about continuing that practice. In contemporary terms, it is a complete lifestyle change from selfishness to doing as God directs; from independence to submission.

If your choices are changing, you are repenting. If you are at this place in your life, then you can recognize what repentance there is in your heart, soul, mind, and body. As you turn away from the old, turn to God. Remove the sin, and fill the space with righteousness.

Sometimes, we are only capable of changing ourselves with God's help.

It was very simple for me; I was to believe in and follow God's Word and promises, and I would be forgiven. This sounds simple, but it was difficult for me to put my complete trust and faith in His Word because people in whom I had put my trust and faith had failed me. How much harder it was to trust almighty God to love me unconditionally. I had to come to the place where I could choose to surrender my life to God and relinquish my control of everything to Him.

This is salvation. It is simple, but it takes more courage than any other human activity, including war and martyrdom. Submission to an unseen, unknown, and unproven God takes a leap of faith that is unrivaled in life.

So what's keeping you from submitting to God? You?

> The people living in darkness have seen a great light; on those living in the land of the shadow of

death a light has dawned. From that time on Jesus
began to preach, "Repent, for the kingdom of heaven
is near." (Matthew 4:16–17)

Those who are sitting in the darkness of their sin can see the light
of the Lord if they choose to. Repentance is choosing or intending to
turn away from that sin to what God would have us do.

Are you ready and able to take that leap of faith?

God's expectations of us are clear. The following Bible verses
explain what He demands of us:

Repent of this wickedness and pray to the Lord.
Perhaps he will forgive you for having such a
thought in your heart. (Acts 8:22)

Ask forgiveness! As hard as it may seem to be, it is rewarding to
have done it. To be forgiven of even the "little" sins we have releases
us from our self-torment and torture. It frees us from the tyranny of
Satan and strengthens our resolve to follow the will of God alone.

That if you confess with your mouth, "Jesus is
Lord," and believe in your heart that God raised him
from the dead, you will be saved. (Romans 10:9)

This is believing. This is knowing in your heart that the Lord
Jesus is with you and will not leave you for any reason, except that
you send him away. Please don't send him away.

To redeem is to buy back. Christ has bought us back.

If we confess our sins, he is faithful and just and
will forgive us our sins and purify us from all
unrighteousness. (1 John 1:9)

Receive this freedom in Christ, even if it takes time. This may
be easier said than done; sometimes it takes much time and effort.
Receiving the full benefit of the Lord in our lives seems strange to us
sometimes, and we may struggle with accepting that it can happen.

We can learn to accept it and believe it. Over time and with many subtle encouragements from the Lord, we will see and believe that he is the Lord of our lives.

> And we have seen and testify that the Father has sent his Son to be the Savior of the world. (1 John 4:15)

See? I told you so. The Lord will dwell in your heart if you let Him. So let Him—even ask Him to do.

> I tell you, whoever acknowledges me before men, the Son of Man will also acknowledge him before the angels of God. (Luke 12:8)

This is not just for this life but also the next. Eternity with God seems much more appealing to me than the alternative. It is possible for each of us who is willing.

If you are unsure of what to do and how to do it, let the Lord lead you. Even though many can give you direction, it's the Lord who walks with you through the changes and growth in life. Spiritual growth needs spiritual help. Turn to Him and stay with Him as you travel this road.

**This Is Doable!**

The cross is the pivotal point, the turning place, where life truly begins.

God is the judge, and I pled my case with Him. God accepted me with open, loving arms and unconditional love. I pled my case before Him, always with Jesus by my side.

If you are afraid of going before the judge yourself, alone, realize that Jesus is always by your side if you call upon His name. Our loving God and friend Jesus Christ will not treat you any differently than He treated me.

> But now, this is what the LORD says—he who created you, O Jacob, he who formed you, O Israel: "Fear not, for I have redeemed you, I have summoned

you by name; you are mine. When you pass through the waters, I will be with you; and when you pass through the rivers, they will not sweep over you. When you walk through the fire, you will not be burned; the flames will not set you ablaze. For I am the LORD your God, the Holy One of Israel, your Savior." (Isaiah 43:1–3)

True repentance is a process. It can be a very slow process for some; it was for me. I struggled with the true meaning of repentance. I stayed in a repentant mode for many years, much longer than God required, but Satan was happy to have me there; it stunted my spiritual growth.

Repentance also can be a quick event for some. Whatever the speed or mode, repent of your sinfulness and enter into righteousness with Christ in your life.

Here's the chart again. It may help you understand what has been happening in your life since addressing your past. The boldest section is where we are in the process and in this book. The others are places where we have dwelled, passed through, or aimed for. Where are you? Are you here yet?

| The Process of Repentance | | | | |
|---|---|---|---|---|
| Sin | Remorse | Repentance | Working Repentance | Righteousness |
| our will | | | | God's will |
| absence of repentance | initial repentance | recognition of repentance | repentance at work | fullness of repentance |
| ← | \ | ↑ | / | → |
| Direction of focus | | | | |

Basic repentance, where we are here, is one side of the moment of conversion. This is the turning point. The next chapter discusses the other side—what immediately follows conversion. Let's go see.

# SECTION II

# AT THE CROSS

TRUE SALVATION:

# RESTORATIVE CHOICE

My sister came to me one day, long ago, and in her excitement asked me what I was reading. When I told her, she said I had to put it down and read the book that she had been reading—a book about end times, according to the author's interpretation of the Bible. My sister had found Jesus and wanted desperately to share Him with me. That was the beginning of my search through the Bible for answers to fix myself.

The process of looking for salvation began. I must confess that it took me a while to fully grasp what Jesus had done for me.

You already may have done this, but going through this again will reaffirm your choices. It helps you to know where you are so you can move on to the next steps accordingly. Review never hurts.

Salvation is simply being saved. It is that moment of choice, leaving an old, self-focused way of life to enter a new God-focused way. The way is through Jesus, the Messiah.

If being saved is rescue from danger, then, with Christ, it is being rescued from the danger of damnation to the peace and safety of God. Let's lay it out for you; then you can decide whether it's the path you want to take.

Romans 3:23 tells us, "For all have sinned, and fall short of the glory of God." We have, you know. Each one of us has sinned in different ways. Sin is doing things God does not want us to do, and we have all done some of that. We are a rather independent bunch. Those sins are the things that separate us from God in our relationship with Him.

We all have a relationship with God. Here's how: whether we think it so or not, God created us and set all things in motion. Whether we follow Him or agree with Him or not, we are linked with God. And whether we like it or not, that is a relationship. It may be a broken one, but it is still a relationship.

We also are accountable to God. That simply means that we must answer for our reactions to His commands. If we disobey, or sin, we will have to answer for that in payment. The payment for sin is our lives, not here on earth but the life eternal that could have been with Him in paradise. It is a debt we can never pay. Instead, we will be in the unending, unbearable discomfort of hell in death. In disobedience, it will be without Him and definitely not in paradise. If we obey, we will answer in the obedience itself.

Because we have all disobeyed in some way, we all owe Him for that disobedience. I am sorry to say that we are unable to pay the price and survive. The price is eternity apart from God, separated from Him, in the depths of hell.

Only a perfect man could pay the price, but only a perfect man would not have to pay. Although he would be the only one who could, he would also be the only one who would not need to.

There was such a man. His name is Jesus. He was so perfect that He did pay the price and it was sufficient for you and me and everyone else.

Romans 6: 23 says that "the wages of sin is death." Yes, that's what we deserve for the sin.

That was the price Jesus paid for us! It says so in Romans 5:8—"But God demonstrates his own love for us in this: While we were still sinners, Christ died for us."

Wow!

How do we access this salvation? How do we become a friend of Jesus? Again, "if you confess with your mouth 'Jesus is Lord,' and believe in your heart that God raised him from the dead, you will be saved" (Romans 10: 9). Be truthful when you do this. He knows the difference.

Romans 12:2a says, "Do not conform any longer to the pattern of this world, but be transformed by the renewing of your mind." That is obedience to God. That is also a restoration, by choice, of the relationship you have with God.

Is restoration possible for someone as bad as me?

I still remember asking Jesus to be my Savior, while knowing I was a sinner. I sat at the gate a long time before I could continue. I knew that continuing meant looking at myself even more closely. That was frightening for me. How could I renew my mind after all the wrong things I had done? How could I be restored after where I had been, let alone be good, acceptable, and perfect?

You can't be bad and good, unacceptable and acceptable, or flawed and perfect at the same time. Only with God is recovery possible.

> Jesus looked at them and said, "With man this is impossible, but with God all things are possible."
> (Matthew 19:26)

Mark 9:23, speaking to a man and to me:

> "'If you can'?" said Jesus. "Everything is possible for him who believes."

Although many good-intentioned folks will say no or, at minimum, "It's a stretch to think so," I am here to prove it is possible to heal and move on with God. I will even go as far as to say it is just as possible for you as it is for the greatest of saints—maybe even more so.

Proof No. 1

> Now one of the Pharisees invited Jesus to have dinner with him, so he went to the Pharisee's house and reclined at the table. When a woman who had lived a sinful life in that town learned that Jesus was eating at the Pharisee's house, she brought an alabaster jar of perfume, and as she stood behind him at his feet weeping, she began to wet his feet with her tears. Then she wiped them with her hair, kissed them and poured perfume on them.

When the Pharisee who had invited him saw this, he said to himself, "If this man were a prophet, he would know who is touching him and what kind of woman she is—that she is a sinner."

Jesus answered him, "Simon, I have something to tell you."

"Tell me, teacher," he said.

"Two men owed money to a certain moneylender. One owed him five hundred denarii, and the other fifty. Neither of them had the money to pay him back, so he cancelled the debts of both. Now which of them will love him more?"

Simon replied, "I suppose the one who had the bigger debt cancelled."

"You have judged correctly," Jesus said.

Then he turned toward the woman and said to Simon, "Do you see this woman? I came into your house. You did not give me any water for my feet, but she wet my feet with her tears and wiped them with her hair. You did not give me a kiss, but this woman, from the time I entered, has not stopped kissing my feet. You did not put oil on my head, but she has poured perfume on my feet. Therefore, I tell you, her many sins have been forgiven—for she loved much. But he who has been forgiven little loves little."

Then Jesus said to her, "Your sins are forgiven."

The other guests began to say among themselves, "Who is this who even forgives sins?"

Jesus said to the woman, "Your faith has saved you; go in peace." (Luke 7: 36–50)

The woman sinned much, was forgiven much, and, therefore, was loved much.

This reminds me of Luke 12:48, where Jesus said,

But the one who does not know and does things deserving punishment will be beaten with few blows. From everyone who has been given much, much will be demanded; and from the one who has been entrusted with much, much more will be asked.

This is true, even in grace.

The woman who washed Jesus's feet had come face-to-face with Christ—with His mercy, love, and grace. All I see in this passage is her overwhelming love for Christ; her full acceptance of who He was and what He had done for her. Her faith in Christ is the one and only thing that could heal her. She recognized that He was blessing her for her faith.

This passage brings me back to Isaiah 55:8, where we read that God's ways are not our ways. Jesus acknowledged that the woman was a sinner but an honest, repentant sinner. Her actions proved to Jesus—and to us—where her heart truly was.

On the other hand, the Pharisee in Luke 7 could represent some of our human reactions to other, "greater" sinners. Again, we judge when we shouldn't. We judge the size of sins when no size applies. We judge values when there are none. There are no greater sinners.

In many ways, Christianity is a mirror image, or reverse image, of our human ways. It looks the same, but everything is reversed. We still do many of the same things but with different motives and expectations.

This judgment of sin is an example of one of those mirror images, and even when we see the image through the lens of Christianity, we distort it with a human influence. We are not to judge the sin of another person. It is for God to judge and Him alone.

Let God unwarp the mirror.

God's way is to forgive truly repentant sinners. Our human tendency is to try to hold them accountable when it is not our responsibility. God is capable of this without our help.

Proof No. 2

Unforgivable sin does not show up in the King James Version of the Bible, nor in several other versions.

That amazes me! I had a list of unforgivable sins. My name was on the unforgivable-sins list, but Jesus took it off and entered it in the book of life instead.

Proof No. 3

Jesus is asked,

> "Who then can be saved?"
> Jesus looked at them and said, "With man this is impossible, but not with God; all things are possible with God." (Mark 10:26–27)

If all things are possible, then restoration is possible for you and everyone you know!
The process is:

- Confess that you are a sinner, and confess that sin.
- Ask forgiveness for your sin.
- Ask Jesus Christ to come into your life and live in you.
- Live for Him.
- Thank God.
- Praise God!

If you are not willing to go through these steps, you will never find forgiveness, peace, and freedom. God does not force us, and we have to be willing to step up and have a desire strong enough to keep going, even if it's tough.

Mark 9:23 again—"'If you can'?" said Jesus. "Everything is possible for him who believes."

Our God will not lead us down a path we cannot follow. He

will not put anything before us for which He has not given us the wherewithal to deal with it.

Again, Matthew 19:26—"Jesus looked at them and said, 'With man this is impossible, but with God all things are possible.'" Believe this, and continue on.

## ASKING FORGIVENESS:

# SUBMISSIVE CHOICE

Society sets a trap for us by implying that one major mistake makes us evil at heart. The victims of this lie spring the trap on themselves by believing it, instead of believing the Word of God.

Forget this lie! Again, watch out for Satan's deceiving ways.

Then seek forgiveness from God *first*!

God does not forgive you if you don't admit you have sinned— each sin and each detail of the sin. Admission comes with remorse and is the first part of repentance.

Forgiveness does not erase the wrong done, nor does it deem the deed acceptable. Forgiveness excuses the sinner from the punishment for the sin.

One truth I discovered through this journey is that God does not release us from the burden of sin until we acknowledge it completely to ourselves and before His throne. Trying to minimize what we have done does not work with God. He knows the truth. He wants the whole truth and nothing but the truth. Interestingly, He already knows but wants us to face up to our own guilt and to admit it to ourselves and to Him.

My abortion has been the most embarrassing part of my being, the innermost secret part of my soul. Opening myself up for God to completely see me as an open book was very intimidating, and I felt very vulnerable.

It is the same when we open up to people, only the reaction seems more immediate.

The fear of being rejected was *almost* unbearable, but I chose to allow Him to see it all—my stupidity, my emotions, and my guilt, as I saw it.

Once I accomplished laying before God every intricate detail that my abortion encompassed, and I fully accepted the truth of His Word, God could do a work in me. By *every intricate detail*, I include the realization that I had actually taken another person's life. My selfishness of not wanting to ruin my life in whatever capacity that was and the fear of telling my parents and boyfriend were some of the details. Not being able to admit to myself and others how I got pregnant was an overwhelming issue to deal with, which was ultimately the reason I carried out the second wrong choice, the abortion.

I have almost relived the whole experience but from the baby's point of view. The emotional pain was difficult, somewhat like letting the poison out of a huge sore, but very cleansing at the same time. These were some of the details I had to lay before my Creator, God. While talking to God about these things, I could envision myself laying these issues down at the foot of the cross. That's what I mean by *laying before God*.

Immaturity and irresponsibility were also vital factors that needed to be addressed before coming to God.

We often suppress critical, traumatic events in our lives as a survival attempt. When events occur with which we are neither mature nor responsible enough to cope, our minds justify the circumstances sufficiently to bury any emotional or spiritual repercussions. In simple terms, we hide the truth until we are old enough to handle it. A few are old enough already, a few never become old enough, and the rest mature at widely varying rates.

As our persons—minds, emotions, and spirits—are able to cope, we slowly realize the scope of what took place. The realization of taking another person's life, in this case, was a big step in the process. Once realized, it needed to be laid before God.

We have to go beyond just believing to having faith in God's

Word. We must claim His Word and all He did on the cross to pay for our sin. Forgiveness is the first part, followed by cleansing and restoration.

This is so powerful because through this realization of what took place and the healing found in Jesus, the focus became less about me and more about Jesus Christ. If I am supposed to be a mirror image of Jesus, I must look like Him and not me. Forgiveness is from His grace—His free gift to us. That is most important, not what I can do to gain it. Amazing!

All the efforts we put into doing something good enough to cover our sin is commendable, but it is only cheating God. We are, in essence, saying we can do something great enough to cover our wrongs. Not possible. No amount of good we do can pay for the wrong, only Christ can do that. We are not fully recognizing or acknowledging who Jesus is and what price He paid for our redemption if we try to save ourselves.

Is it any wonder there are so many Christians who do not live victorious lives? How can they? Instead of praising Jesus for what He has done, they are consumed with doing enough good to do it themselves.

God wants us to be obedient to Him. *Christian* means Christ follower, not Christ leader. He is the leader; we are to follow. Doing things on our own does not fit into the follower category.

God is a jealous God. No credit is due us for our salvation because nothing we do helps. Jesus alone is our Redeemer.

There are two basic reasons for doing something: obligation or desire. If we do something only because we feel under obligation to do it, then we do not agree with it. Our motives, in this case, are not honest or honoring to God. However, if we do something because we want to, we express agreement and approval of the activity. This is honoring to God, as long as it is something of which He would approve or something He has asked of us.

Even if what we are doing is a good thing, if we are not doing it for the right reason, we should not be doing it at all, or at least we should check our motives.

I have noticed, over the years, that I have become less judgmental of others and more accepting and loving of them, just as they are— at least, I have improved. This is because I know God sees me as His child, covered by the blood of Christ, and I can extend this to not judging others. This has made a significant difference to me as a person because I know that, in itself, it's only a by-product of finding freedom through Jesus. There is no longer the need to justify myself before God. There is a great peace in finding that I am more understanding, accepting, and loving of others, of being able to see them as God sees them.

Being judgmental is watered-down language for not forgiving. Being judgmental is simply not forgiving.

After seeking forgiveness from God first, then seek forgiveness from yourself next.

What is a good person? I often heard my parents refer to a neighbor in our community as being a good person and that surely she was going to heaven because she was a good person.

I have struggled with this concept for a long time because my abortion took me completely off the good-person list and left me with feelings of belonging on the unacceptable-person list.

I have friends who are beautiful women and great servants of God who suffer from not feeling good enough. They also suffer from depression. What a trap Satan has us in. They are good people.

How depressing—we may have a hard time not falling into depression when we do all we can to get on the good-person list but never make it. Is it any wonder that when we try so hard, we come out feeling so defeated?

How could I ever rise above the unacceptable-person sensation with feelings of never being able to see myself as a *good* person? God calls us to be holy and perfect as Christ is holy and perfect.

Do nothing out of selfish ambition or vain conceit, but in humility consider others better than yourselves. (Philippians 2:3)

Be holy, because I am holy. (1 Peter 1:16)

Bible verses such as these left me struggling between trying to do good things to climb the social ladder of life and trusting God to lead me. It left me at the mercy of others who dictated what I needed to do on a daily basis because I thought they knew better than I did. All the while, I was trying to be a good person in the sight of God. I found myself in a trap of too many priorities. I found that as far as it involved me or my family, everybody else came before me.

On several occasions, I sat down and made a list of what my priorities were, and I realized that my kids, husband, and especially me came last on the list. This was wrong. There was no healthy balance in any attempt I made. I was always left feeling empty, regardless of all my attempts.

I had a very distorted view of people as a whole. A healthy balance allows a healthy set of priorities, where an individual's needs are met, as well as the needs of others.

Riding on being a *good person* (by society's definition) can be very dangerous. No good person is good all the time, except Jesus Christ. Satan can fool many people into thinking they are good enough and that they don't need Jesus Christ in their lives. We need to come to terms with ourselves before God about being a sinner—as we are told in Roman 3:23:"For all have sinned, and fall short of the glory of God"—not about how good we are. This may be much more difficult if a person is a good person at heart anyway.

Just as evil people can do good things, so can good people do evil things. We all have weaknesses.

While I dealt with my abortion, I looked at myself very closely and found motives that were impure in other areas—coveting other people's things or lives, being judgmental of others, and other things. Some of my sins were invisible, and other people did not know, but I realized God knew. The more I became aware of my sinful nature, the more I knew how much I needed God's forgiveness for many things, not just one. The more I poured out myself at the foot of the cross, the more I realized just how much Jesus Christ must love me to die for all those sins.

Our motives should be checked constantly as to why we may choose (yes, there is a choice) to do or not do anything that comes up. Our ultimate purpose for doing good things should be for the glory of God. I eventually realized that anything I was doing and resenting accomplished nothing to glorify God. If I resented anything, I took it off the list. The list shrank!

> For it is by grace you have been saved, through faith—and this not from yourselves, it is the gift of God—not by works, so that no one can boast. For we are God's workmanship, created in Christ Jesus to do good works, which God prepared in advance for us to do. (Ephesians 2:8–10)

You can work yourself to the bone, but then, you are trying to accomplish your own ends, not God's. Ephesians 2:8–9 says that you can work all you want at saving yourself, but you will accomplish nothing because God is not interested in what you can do. He wants you to acknowledge that it is His grace that covers your sin. Otherwise, He is not the one being glorified. It's really about who are you willing to allow to be glorified.

It's so simple; we are the ones who complicate it.

Our efforts are a form of boasting. Boasting can be as simple as leaning or relying on the good we are doing to make ourselves look and feel better about ourselves.

> But, "Let him who boasts boast in the Lord." For it is not the one who commends himself who is approved, but the one whom the Lord commends. (2 Corinthians 10:17–18)

God showed me His ways, and He did not want me to lean on my good works and deeds to be acceptable to Him. If I cannot boast about any of my good works, then they are redundant, useless, and of no value whatsoever to God. So there goes the social ladder of life.

All of a sudden, the priority list was all gone.

There was less of me and more of Him, almost like weighing myself on a scale. Less of me and more of He who paid the price, so that when I stand in front of God, He sees Jesus, not me. The greater the sinner I saw in myself, the greater love I saw Jesus having for me. The more my love for Jesus grew, the more I wanted to serve Him.

As you empty yourself of yourself, in favor of God, you will be filled with Him. You will learn to die to yourself, and you will have a deep desire to become holy and perfect, as God is perfect.

I also found out I cannot do this on my own. I need God's help to accomplish this.

*Perfect* is a matter of perspective. Our perspective of perfection is based on the model of the world. God's perspective of perfection is based on His Son, Jesus.

> Be perfect, therefore, as your heavenly Father is
> perfect. (Matthew 5:48)

This is a command of God!

> Because by one sacrifice he has made perfect forever
> those who are being made holy. (Hebrews 10:14)

The offering of Jesus, the Son of God, on the cross for our transgressions sanctifies those who fully turn to God for forgiveness and restoration of a relationship with Him. His perfection for our salvation.

I finally could get out of the good-person trap—that trap of thinking I needed to be a good person to earn my way into God's grace. Jesus is the only perfect one. Randy says, "Stop being the good person! It isn't helping and won't help. You can't do it. Only

Jesus could and did for you. Be Christlike, not good on your own power."

This *good* is the good we do to try to gain something. It is the good we do to earn our own way, rather than rely on the way God provided through Jesus the Messiah. This kind of good is not going to help our case in any way. In fact, it may hinder it. This kind of good may lead us away from serving a risen Savior to serving ourselves only. What a tragedy this is when it happens.

Being a good person is an attempt at balancing the wrong things we have done with the good. It's our way of trying to pay for our sins.

Now, the things I do are not to make myself look good but to glorify God. He has set me free, and I accomplish things to serve Him and give Him the honor and glory because of my love and gratitude to Him. "Therefore I glory in Christ Jesus in my service to God" (Romans 15:17).

I know the sin I have committed, and I know that my total honesty with God has led to freedom and allowed me to once again feel like an authentic, honest, and good person. I feel like a person who has allowed herself to see that she was a sinner, like every other human being God has created and allowed free will; definitely no more and no less a sinner.

Suddenly, I can see that we are all at the same place—on our knees before God.

The following passage is an encouragement to me that I am set free:

> Once you were alienated from God and were enemies in your minds because of your evil behavior. But now he has reconciled you by Christ's physical body through death to present you holy in his sight, without blemish and free from accusation. (Colossians 1:21–22)

I can become holy because of Christ's death and Resurrection.

He died to present me holy in His sight, without blemish and free from accusation.

Hebrews 10:10 says, "And by that will, we have been made holy through the sacrifice of the body of Jesus Christ once for all." We have been made holy through the death of Jesus Christ, once and for all. We have not been made holy out of our own doing.

With time, I understood Isaiah 55:8–9, which says,

> "For my thoughts are not your thoughts, neither are your ways my ways," declares the LORD. "As the heavens are higher than the earth, so are my ways higher than your ways and my thoughts than your thoughts."

With His help, I was set free from the good-person syndrome. The chains came off, one by one, when I grasped the concept that I am not a good person; I am a sinner. I was a sinner long before the abortion. I am now covered by the blood of Christ, and I am pleasing and acceptable to God.

I did eventually come to terms with the fact that I am not good, but Christ who covers me is perfect, releasing me from having to be perfect ahead of time. I rely on Him for my salvation, and any good in me is credited to Christ alone. I strive to be perfect because He is perfect, and He is my Lord.

After seeking forgiveness from God first and then seeking forgiveness from self next, then seek forgiveness from family and friends.

I was raised in a family that held high moral standards and valued honesty. Until I told them, I felt as though I was living a double standard, a lie. I needed their forgiveness. I believe this is why I wanted to shout from the rooftop the truth about my abortion. I also believe that not truly feeling free to do that made me feel like a liar, when, in actuality, I struggled because, deep down, I was an honest person.

When I share with others what I did—that is, aborted a baby—I don't necessarily require the person to understand why I chose that path. I just ask that they love me anyhow. That is, I seek acceptance.

Acceptance can only come when forgiveness is granted. By confessing the sin, we imply that we are asking for forgiveness. When acceptance is extended, forgiveness is implied.

This does not work with God. We must confess to Him *and* ask forgiveness. It does work with people, through generally understood rules of communication. While not foolproof, it's usually successful.

I am not saying we need to make our sin known to everyone we encounter. I could share what I did with someone, and they might give me momentary relief but only that. But there are some people we need to tell and others who don't need to know.

It was my total honesty before God that set me free. As nice as it is to be acceptable to others, they don't have the power to set us free from our sin and guilt. God, on the other hand, can set it as far as the east is from the west, and He completely forgets it—or sets it aside—unless we bring it up.

To encourage you, I will leave you with this fact: God is more understanding and loving than humans. Deal with Him, and He will lead you where you need to go. His grace far surpasses the grace people show.

Now, let's rebuild with new materials.

SELF-CONSTRUCTION:

# RECONSTRUCTIVE CHOICE

As we forgive ourselves, we must move on to reconstruct who we are and how we see ourselves.

Through this process, we can become who we should be in the hands of the Lord. We can follow the mold Jesus laid out for us and become as much like Him as possible.

*Christian* means Christlike as well as Christ follower. To become Christlike, some alterations are needed. Those alterations are the reconstruction, or renovation, necessary in each of us. No matter what our past, our mistakes, or our choices have been, we are not like Christ until we turn to Him and turn to be like Him.

Prior to giving our lives to Christ, we see ourselves in mirrors that are warped. Our view of ourselves is distorted into a false image of who we are. Often, that image is so far distorted from reality that there is no corrective lens that can show Christ. We can make no connection between the image we see and the one we would like to see—that of Jesus.

It's only when the mirror has been "unwarped" that it's possible to see a glimpse of Jesus or to see the possibility that He might appear in us or through us. Our warped view of ourselves can leave us feeling so far from Christlikeness that reaching it seems impossible.

I thank God that He can unwarp our mirrors.

God's grace—have you tasted it today? Have you savored it in each fiber of your being? Have you bathed in His unconditional love? Have you been washed in His precious blood? Have you come forth out of the pool of sin with such enthusiasm that you know He has touched you? Have you touched His robe as He passed by, knowing by faith alone that He is touching you? Is His grace overflowing in you? Have you been filled by the living water that cleanses through and through? Has God made you brand new so when you look at yourself in the mirror, you are a reflection of Him—a pool of still water? Are you reflecting Him because of Him?

The above phrases express some of what the Lord calls us to be and do. They are things mentioned in the Bible that we can reach in our lives by turning to the Lord for our strength and our lead. Look through the Word of God, and find the ones that speak to you.

The aim in this process is to turn away from focusing solely on ourselves to become a servant of God in attitude and deed. And we will do this for no other reason than for God to get the glory. There will be no selfish motive or earthly gain intended. All this is because we have come to an understanding of what Christ did for us on the cross. We believe He paid for our sin, and now we have a desire to see Jesus's name lifted rather than ours.

This is where the reconstruction comes in. We must be careful, though. We can do this according to the will of God, or we can go off on our own again and maybe become better people but still not be true followers of the Lord Jesus Christ.

We may look at ourselves and wonder if there are any changes taking place in us. I saw no change in myself until I visited an old friend. She was still living in the old ways, and I wasn't there anymore. It was more than the changes that come with marriage, children, and the events of life; it was a deep change in who I was and how I was defined. The changes were subtle but clear. God sometimes changes us slowly. I have discovered that He isn't in a hurry, especially when He is molding His children.

Sometimes, the change in us will be so obvious to others that they will comment. Other times, they may not recognize the changes, and only we can see them in comparison to our old selves. They can still be profound when we look at them.

I often look in awe at God's creation—the sunsets, the sunrises, the autumn display of wondrous colors, the freshness of the new array of green leaves, the fish and the birds, along with much more. I find myself saying, "What a great painting God has made." Imagine—for one moment or longer, if necessary, until it truly soaks into your innermost being—how we will be painted into His picture. This is not by ourselves but by the hand of almighty God, and we will be even more glorious to God than any of His other creation.

If God can cause such beauty as the sunset with a simple stroke of the brush, wouldn't He do a work in us that surpasses all the beauty in the world? He has the rest of our lives to do it. Think of what we will be worth when He has worked on us. What self-worth we will feel as a masterpiece of God's.

It may seem insignificant, but saying no—or, more specifically, being unable to say no—can be one side effect of our self-worth. When we have made bad choices with severe consequences, our self-worth dwindles to nothing. We quickly learn to distrust our own decision-making abilities and rely on others to tell us what we need to do. Eventually, there is a tendency to think we are nothing and that others are far better than we are. In submission to their superiority, we cannot say no to their requests.

By walking through steps of growth with the Lord and following His will for us, we can return to a belief that we too have value and worth in His eyes. You can reach this place of self-worth, of decision-making, and of being able to say no.

At the same time, you will find yourself in a place of complete honesty and openness with your heavenly Father—a place of comfort of being who He created you to be; a place where you are walking and talking together.

There is nothing quite like sharing your deepest secrets with your spouse and, sometimes, special friends and having them love, support, and accept you, regardless of circumstances. Your love for each other is affirmed and solidified. It's the same way with God. You can approach Him openly, even in your anger, and rest assured He is still there for you. You will find yourself in His presence more often and love to be there. You no longer will feel condemned or that you have to measure up. It will be as if your eyes are fully opened for the first time, knowing He loves you unconditionally, and all He wants in return is your love for Him and His people.

That's what makes God awesome!

It breaks my heart to see that this does not always happen with each other. Our spouses, being human, may not be ready or able to be the loving, supportive, and accepting person we so desperately need. God will provide someone to walk with you, but it may not be who you would expect or hope for. It may not even be someone you want, but it will be someone who loves you and is willing to listen to you and walk with you through this time. Be open to whomever it may be.

I find myself very contented with who I am because I am who God created. I forever strive to be more like Jesus, but I can still allow myself to be in the place where I have to keep on trying.

This is just one of the ways we can rebuild our self-esteem. We can come to a place of believing again that God made us the way He wanted us. We may have doubted Him and messed up, but He can forgive, and we can move on. We can grow from our past or pass on our growth—God gives us the choice.

We must demolish the old self with its sinful tendencies. This leaves some empty spaces in our lives. Those spaces are subject to being filled with sin again, unless we fill them with righteousness first. "Seek first the kingdom of God" means fill up with Him, and all better things will be given to you. There will be no room for sin to regain a foothold.

God made each of us a precious jewel. Let Him polish that jewel to shine for Him.

The friends I've made since becoming a follower of Christ Jesus think I have always been like I am now. They didn't know the old, carnal me. This is a clear indication to me that I have indeed changed from who I once was.

I want it known that I was a sinner, saved by grace, and that I am a child of God so that I may reach others and share God's grace.

## "IT IS FINISHED":

# ACCEPTANCE CHOICE

> When he had received the drink, Jesus said, "*It is finished.*"
> With that, he bowed his head and gave up his spirit.
> —John 19:30 (emphasis added)

The Greek language from which we translate that verse uses only one word for what Jesus said. *It is finished* is a single utterance, ending His mission to the world. He completed everything He had come to do on the cross. He completed paying for our sin.

I could list all the details of every sin ever committed, but what would that accomplish? The end is all the same; we have sinned against God. No one needs to be reminded of what they have done; we already know. You may be dealing with other issues, but God sees those as well and helps equally with them.

Let's think about the details of how the entire human race put Jesus to death on the cross because of our sin. He died for the sin of the world.

Jesus Christ had victory over death on the cross, and with Him, we can have victory over the sin in our lives.

> Because by one sacrifice he has made perfect forever
> those who are being made holy. The Holy Spirit also
> testifies to us about this. First he says: "This is the
> covenant I will make with them after that time, says
> the Lord. I will put my laws in their hearts, and
> I will write them on their minds." Then he adds:

"Their sins and lawless acts I will remember no more." (Hebrews 10:14–17)

Jesus knew why and for whom He was going to the cross. He could look ahead in time and see that humankind's only hope was through His choice to die on the cross. He could also look ahead and see me and what I was guilty of. He could see you too. He knew us each by name. He also knew we had no hope without Him.

When Jesus Christ died, He uttered, "It is finished" (John 19:30). He accomplished something that no other could do; He paid for our sin in full. Jesus chose to go to hell so humankind did not have to go there for eternity. We, in turn, have to acknowledge that.

**Jesus loves each of us that much.**

I can picture myself at the foot of the cross, thousands of years ago. I know my presence there was not just as an onlooker; I took part in crucifying Him. I also actively took part when He rose again on the third day for my freedom.

Jesus died for humanity's redemption, as John 19:30 declares.

Somewhere along the way, the consequences of our decisions catch up to us. For me, it was when I had children. What I had done became real. I had a daily reminder, looking into the faces of my beautiful children.

That is when my actions, my decision to abort a "problem" became murdering a human being. When I looked at my children, I could not deny the facts.

But when I die, Jesus will greet me at heaven's gate. I envision that He will be holding my baby in His arms. He won't love me less because of my sin. He will love me despite my sin.

You see, when God looks at sin—whether small or big, according to human standard—it is still sin. He died not only for my action but for the guilt and the shame—and that is truly amazing. I am free because of the great I AM.

Where are you in grace giving? When you can freely give it, you have truly received it.

> As you go, preach this message: "The kingdom of heaven is near." Heal the sick, raise the dead, cleanse those who have leprosy, drive out demons. Freely you have received, freely give. (Matthew 10:7–8)

When God's grace touches your innermost being, you become a grace-giver, no longer a grace-grabber. Grace-grabbers are those who think they deserve grace, freedom, and life eternal, based on who they are and that no one else deserves it. They grab for themselves and keep without giving or sharing.

> We cannot give what we do not have. We do not have until we receive. When Jesus says to each one of us, "It is finished," we have received our freedom in Him. In gratitude and love, sharing the gift becomes the need in us. That is when we become grace-givers.

What a place to be. Pray that God empowers you to believe His Word and the power in it. You are not alone; you are part of an army that seeks to be all that God intended for us to be.

I pray that Satan's lies will dissipate as the cages of our lives disappear, and we are set free—free to be God-revering.

I've often wondered what a *reverent fear* of God is. I believe it's acknowledging who God is and realizing that He is capable of anything. He can choose to destroy us or fight for us. I had an unhealthy fear of God for years, but as I discovered His truth and grace, I better understood reverent fear.

> The fear of the LORD is the beginning of wisdom;
> all who follow his precepts have good understanding.
> To him belongs eternal praise. (Psalm 111:10)

I used to fear God in such a way that I was scared He would find me out and want to punish me and therefore squish me. The Bible says, "Your sin will find you out" (Numbers 32:23). We can be sure of this. Maybe not in this life, but in the next, our sin will expose us. In this passage, Moses implies that their sin will eventually bring its own punishment. Ours will too. There is freedom in letting God in on *all* your secrets.

I have assurance that God has the power to squish me, if that is His desire (I acknowledge this), and it's OK. I can fully rest in His hand, and I am forever safe there. If squishing me is part of His plan, I'm OK with that, for "if God is for [me], who can be against [me]?" (Romans 8:31).

Knowing our place in the larger scheme of things helps us relate to God properly.

Many people who fly have witnessed perspective. When we sit close to someone, that person appears to be the same size, approximately, as we are. Looking down from thirty-five thousand feet, it's extremely difficult to discern a car, let alone a person. Our perspective from high in the air is that people are very small; therefore, they seem insignificant.

God is our Master Creator. He is more than all His creation and all the universe. In that perspective, we are not as significant or important as we would like to think we are. Yet He still chose us as His favorite out of all His creation.

Reverence grows from that perspective.

It amazes me to think of God's love for me and you. His love is so far beyond our comprehension.

I close my eyes and allow myself to be in the presence of God— and God alone—saying nothing, asking nothing, just meditating on my favorite verse: "Be still, and know that I am God" (Psalm 46:10). I imagine myself in a field of tall hay, and I can feel the wind on my back and a peace that surpasses all understanding. I sense I'm under God's wing, and all my concerns of life fade away. Nothing matters because I can sense God's control over all things, not my control.

Why? Because I gave my life to Jesus, good and bad. My life is finished; now it is His.

Give God the tools—the different ways and devices—you have used to try to fix your life and everything in it.

God is the great physician. "For I am the LORD who heals thee" (Exodus 15: 26).

> Jesus answered them, "It is not the healthy who need a doctor, but the sick. I have not come to call the righteous, but sinners to repentance." (Luke 5:31–32)

We only go to a doctor when we realize we are sick. We must realize we are spiritually sick and in need of a spiritual doctor, namely God.

Allow Him to do His great work. Allow Him to heal you. It requires that you give Him control instead of holding on to it yourself. It requires you to believe He is capable. You have to have faith in His ability and recognize who He is. It requires you to have faith enough in God and trust in His Word. If you truly repent, He will forgive you. His grace *is* sufficient.

People's prayers to God are offered in such a way that they themselves still have control of circumstances and answers. When God does not answer the way they want, they feel that God did not hear their prayers. Having stipulations attached to our prayers seems to be only our way of praying. We want prayers answered our way; it seems easier to accept those answers because that's within our realm of faith, control, and understanding.

God, on the other hand, wants us to pray, giving Him all the control. We must have faith enough in God that He will answer the right way, not necessarily our way. When we maintain control, it is often our pride getting in the way of our growth.

Many of the prayers recorded in the Bible are totally selfless. Take the example in Acts 4:24–30. The early church prayed for the misled leaders of the time, the spiritually lost, and the ones who were persecuting them. Our selfish prayers seem so insignificant and inappropriate in light of these prayers of faith.

You will be amazed as God makes you into a new creation. He not only changes our hearts about our situations but also gives us renewed hearts and new lives. The journey to victory has begun.

Once we have repented of our sin, God leaves it at the cross, and so can we. The only time our sin is mentioned again is when we bring it up. He will never bring it up against us.

We don't have to stay at the cross either. We are free to leave Calvary and the cross. We are free to move in our new lives, to grow and become all that God has set out for us to become.

That old life of ours is finished as well. It was finished when we accepted the finished work of the Redeemer. We need to finish going to it and live only in the new life in Jesus.

BELIEF TO FAITH:

# MIGRATING CHOICE

Faith is the same choice as belief—to follow Jesus—but faith is made in the heart as well as in the head, whereas belief is only in the head, our thoughts. Initially, the choice to turn to Christ was a conscious one that was made in the mind. At some subsequent point, it became a choice that also was made in the seat of our emotions and attitudes. We not only know the Lord, but He has become an integral part of us. His will is what we do automatically.

This inclusion of heart with the mind is a migration of the belief to involve all our being. Thus, it is a *migrating choice*. It is moving those few inches from brain to heart, from intellect to emotion.

The word *believe* does not say enough for me. I want to go further; I want to move on to *faith*.

Believing in something or someone does not require anything from you, other than maybe a passing thought. Faith moves you into a new dimension of being actively involved with God. In believing, you might acknowledge that God exists, but faith knows Him personally and claims Him as He truly is—real and alive.

Believing is knowing in your mind that something is true. Faith takes what you believe and reacts to it. Faith in God is putting your life in God's care.

Faith includes belief, whereas belief does not include faith. Belief is cognitive only. Faith is cognitive, affective, and behavioral, all at once. That just means it's in your thoughts, your attitude, and your actions at the same time. It's where we consciously know about the

Lord, desire to follow in His will, and act out as He directs us. Many well-intentioned folks get stuck or stranded at the believing place. They believe there is a God, but they do not do as He asks, nor do they have any desire to do so. They are convinced that they are in God's good graces, and they continue life as they always have. There is no apparent lifestyle change or heart change in them. Their attitude toward life and other people is still selfish.

Faith is the step that is much harder to take than mere belief. It requires something from us. It requires dedication to something other than our own interests. It requires dedication to God.

I attended church as a child and grew up believing there was a God—God the Father; the Son, Jesus; and the Holy Spirit. I feared God more than anything. I never heard in church that God loved us or that He could forgive our sin. The ritual for forgiveness involved my admitting I had done something wrong, and it required an action on my part, but there was no clear connection, that I recall, to Jesus's having died for those sins. I must admit, though, that as a child, I might have missed some of the truths that were taught.

We can go through a lifetime of sitting in church and hearing the gospel truth about Jesus but never make the connection. Transferring from belief to faith is not a matter of following a religion or ritual. Few people have attended a church and not heard about Jesus Christ's life, death, and Resurrection.

For me, believing is knowing the story, and faith is recognizing that I fit into that story. It includes learning that Jesus knew of me when He was crucified more than two thousand years ago.

My new journey with Jesus has taken me to new areas of growth, which called me to new levels of trust. Admittedly, I was cautious and only opened myself up a little at a time. Jesus slowly became my friend. It was easier for me to allow Jesus in than God the Father because I could relate to Jesus's loving me enough to die for my sin. I knew I needed that. God the Father was more intimidating and, I expected, judgmental.

I never felt pressured to grow as a Christian any faster than I could handle or desired. Day by day, I could sense Jesus patiently walking with me.

I accepted Christ as my Savior, but then I got stuck in the works mode; I tried to work off my sins. I was there for a long time and became exasperated, tired, frustrated, and still guilt-ridden for years. I was neither hot nor cold; I was scared of going farther than that because I felt I could not face God. I believed I was saved but no more.

I believe many people are at this place in their salvation. They too need to move on in their faith in God.

Your depth of faith is somewhat dependent on how much you trust God instead of yourself.

Time has allowed me to claim what Jesus did for me, dying on the cross for my sin, as truth, as a genuine act that actually accomplishes what the Bible says it accomplishes—paying for my sin. That is belief. I have set myself aside from the need to be good in the sight of God and have released myself of what I have done wrong—my sin; specifically, my abortion. I have acknowledged and surrendered to the power of the cross to cover sin.

Faith is a step deeper than belief. You do have to believe in order to have faith, though. They work together, head and heart.

They can both be blocked, however. Free will extends to every aspect of our existence. We are free to believe or not. We are free to have faith and to place our faith where we choose. We are also free to choose to hold back our belief and faith when it suits us. Commitment to God is the choice to not hold back our belief or our faith in Him.

If we allow the guilt and shame of sin or hold on to our sin and continually feel bad but never move ahead, it's just as disappointing to God as if we feel too proud of ourselves. Either way, we are not letting God be God; it's still about us. We need to completely take our eyes off ourselves and look at the cross. Then and only then, when it's not about us but about Jesus, will we find complete freedom. (We are still being selfish if we don't acknowledge this.)

As long as we wallow in self-pity, it's still about us. If we blame ourselves, that too is still about us. Take the time to pray and ask Jesus to reveal Himself to you. He will help you move forward. He is always gracious in this.

Instead of wallowing in self-pity, I bathe in my Lord and Savior's forgiveness. I praise Him continually for what He has done. I sing songs. I find myself dancing in His presence when I praise Him and thank Him for what He has done.

Satan does not have much room for attack when we give Jesus all the praise He deserves. When you are under attack, find a chorus you can sing, or put on spiritually uplifting music. When Jesus is present, Satan cannot be.

The *fullness of repentance* takes us to a new level that goes beyond ourselves and into the realm of God. It goes to the place where we allow Jesus to be "the way, the truth, and the life" (John 14:6). This is the place where it's no longer about us but *all* about Jesus. It's the place where we meet the abundant life spoken about in John 10:10—"The thief comes only to steal and kill and destroy; I have come that they may have life, and have it to the full." This is where we find peace with ourselves, joy in this life, and love for our neighbors, enemies, and ourselves.

Simply put, the *fullness of repentance* is a person's entire submission to God. This is not just a consent but a devotion to do all that He has given us to do. It includes repentance of sin, forgiveness of others, the absence of any tendency to evil, and openness to God of all that we are.

I went into the bathroom one day and looked in the mirror. As I looked at myself, I sensed God telling me, *"You are so beautiful."* He was looking at the inner me. At first, I was surprised, but I continued to look at myself and saw myself differently. He unwarped the mirror for me. God was and is the only one who could do that.

His presence was so genuine that it had a life-changing effect on me. I walked away from that mirror, seeing myself as beautiful, like never before. The beauty was as though God was pleased with me, not because I was perfect in any way but because I was His child. There was a new level of transparency and trust with God and in God.

I had always seen Alma as beautiful, simply because she was and still is. Although she has it, not all beauty is on the outside.

When we come to this place of repentance, we again can look at ourselves in the mirror and find beauty in what God has created. We will have a drive to serve others with a joyful heart. We will not serve out of a sense of duty but because we desire to serve others out of love for Christ. We will find the power to say no, when needed. All this will leave us with a song in our hearts, rejoicing over who our Redeemer is. Then we can be a blessing for God.

The apostle Paul chose to be a blessing for God by living a grace-filled life, regardless of his past. We can too.

On the road to Damascus, Paul was transformed by God's touch and by God's grace (Acts 9). He definitely became a new creation in Christ. Amazingly, Paul found God's grace sufficient, and he allowed God's grace to cover all his past. All the Christians he persecuted before he was claimed as one of God's own were still a part of his past.

Discovering Paul's story of persecuting Christians and ordering their deaths helped me understand that even the greatest of people were sinners, just like you and me.

Accepting that God's grace was sufficient to cover Paul's past seems somehow easier for us than trusting that God can do the same for us.

Trust as a child would trust. Childlike faith requires you to just believe without seeing. Just believe without questioning because our questions often have no answers. What better way to glorify God than to trust Him in this measure, without seeing, without questioning.

There's an old saying, "Seeing is believing," but with Christ, seeing is not necessarily believing.

> Then he said to Thomas, "Put your finger here; see
> my hands. Reach out your hand and put it into my
> side. Stop doubting and believe." Thomas said to
> him, "My Lord and my God!" Then Jesus told him,
> "Because you have seen me, you have believed;
> blessed are those who have not seen and yet have
> believed." (John 20:27–29)

Maybe a better way to look at faith is to think that by believing,
we will see. It may sound opposite or reversed but may be more
accurate.

Faith does not require that we understand everything. Again,
faith does not require that we have logically concluded anything. It
is not something we can reason. Faith believes and trusts without
outside proof or evidences. Faith takes what we believe and says,
"In this, I put my trust."

We have many mechanical and electronic devices in our lives
today that we do not necessarily understand—cars, telephones,
computers, dishwashers, and so on. We likely do not know how they
work, but we trust that they do and heavily rely on them in our daily
living. We may not understand them; we may not be able to make
sense of them, but we trust them without needing to know every
detail of their operation or principle of their function.

Aerodynamic principles elude most of us, but we trust airplanes.
Bernoulli's principle is unknown to most, but we trust the carburetors
in our cars that run on his principle. Faith believes and trusts without
outside proof or evidence.

Paul's trust in God's Word must have been uplifting because he
continued to serve God in wonderful ways. That's what God wants
from us. Believing and trusting that God's grace is sufficient is, in
fact, obeying God and showing our love for Him.

> But he said to me, "My grace is sufficient for
> you, for my power is made perfect in weakness."
> Therefore I will boast all the more gladly about my

weaknesses, so that Christ's power may rest on me.
(2 Corinthians 12:9)

When Paul was in prison, he could rejoice in the Lord because he remembered his past. I question whether Paul's thorn in the flesh (2 Corinthians 12:7) was indeed all the memories from his past. Regardless, he could sing to the Lord and be content while in prison because he was very much aware of where he came from and how God's touch changed him.

All of Paul's desires revolved around serving his master in the best way he could, no matter where he was or in what circumstances. Paul stopped beating himself up about where he had been and learned to look at where he was going—home to heaven.

At some point, Paul had to allow God to do what He said He would do—forgive us. God can heal us from the inside out because He deals with our hearts first. Amazingly, God deals with the heart, and He sees all that is in our hearts, yet we worry about the human world, and people do not see the heart. Jesus died to heal the broken-hearted and to forgive their sin and shame.

Paul became very mighty as a servant of God; so can you.

Faith is not entirely blind. When we have gathered sufficient information, we start to believe something is true. When we accept that something as truth, we believe. When we allow that truth to influence our lives in decisions and principles, we are placing our faith in it.

It's that allowance that brings us from the simple belief to faith. We do not have to know every detail about that truth, only that it is true. Allowing it to influence us is, in a sense, submitting to that truth. What better truth to submit to than the truth of our Creator God?

## CONSEQUENTIAL BLESSINGS:

# CLEARER CHOICES

Once we have allowed the influence of truth, we will see more of what that truth holds for us. Among those things we see in truth is an interesting phenomenon—the blessings of God. Our God is so good and loves us so much that He places blessings among the consequences for our choices.

Can you see it? Every time we allow God to show us the true consequences of our actions, we see a blessing clearly standing in the middle of them.

One consequence of extramarital sex is pregnancy and a child. Children are miraculous blessings from God, but that should not be used as an excuse to have extramarital sexual relations. A consequence of committing a crime is incarceration, which can lead to a blessing of rehabilitation and a better life, if it is accepted. Every consequence imposed by God carries a blessing, whether or not we see it, understand it, or accept it.

We may feel that what we have done is too bad for us to be blessed in the midst of it and that we are undeserving. This is stepping into the spiritual realm again, where God's ways and thoughts are not our ways and thoughts. We think it is abnormal to expect blessings in our consequences.

What we feel does not discount the truth of God's love and provision for us. The only consequence that never shows a blessing is the consequence for disbelief. That is separation from God. Separation from the Lord is in no way a good thing. There is no blessing in it.

Have you ever made a mistake that you regret? That could be a sin or just a mistake. The answer, whether you admit it or not, is yes. When others find out about your mistakes, do they comfort you and help you heal and improve, or do they heap more on? Do they add blessings, or do they add curses, saying, "You can't do that," or "You can't participate in this," or "You're not what we want for a church member [or friend or leader]"?

Since when are we designated judge and jury of others? They do not have authority to administer punishments for sin; only God does. Yes, there are government agencies authorized to administer justice and apply the laws of humans, but the law of God is to be administered by God.

> Against you, you only, have I sinned
> and done what is evil in your sight,
> so that you are proved right when you speak
> and justified when you judge. (Psalm 51:4)

We know the rules, and if we don't, we can learn them. God is the Creator and enforcer of His ideals.

We kick and rebel, but His rules are in place only for our benefit. The closer our walks are with God, the more we will understand that our safety, contentment, and true happiness come from being in tune with God's ideals.

God designates a consequence for every action. There is a temporary one—that's here on earth and in our lifetimes—and an eternal one; that's forever. The first one may seem to be eternal and may well last our lifetimes. We really don't understand the last one because we haven't yet seen the blessing in it.

Here is a difficult question you might ask: "What is the blessing in an abortion, and what are its consequences?"

The fact that there are consequences to our decisions in this world is a blessing in itself. I would not want to dream of a world with no consequences, not even for a day. Often, our consequences and consciences are what save us from becoming even more of a threat to ourselves and others. So consequences and, subsequently, our consciences (hopefully) are indeed blessings from God.

If we are honest with ourselves, we realize that no one in our world can follow the Ten Commandments completely for a lifetime. We all suffer from the consequences of bad choices we have made along life's walk.

What we decide to do with our consequences plays a huge part in what and who we become as children of God. We can choose to become better persons because of it or bitter persons. Obviously, a bitter person has no hope of finding joy or peace in that state of mind. I believe that a person who seeks to learn something from their mistakes can often find a more fulfilling life because of it.

The Bible states that we can use our mistakes and the comfort we have from the Lord to comfort others.

> Praise be to the God and Father of our Lord Jesus Christ, the Father of compassion and the God of all comfort, who comforts us in all our troubles, so that we can comfort those in any trouble with the comfort we ourselves have received from God. For just as the sufferings of Christ flow over into our lives, so also through Christ our comfort overflows. If we are distressed, it is for your comfort and salvation; if we are comforted, it is for your comfort, which produces in you patient endurance of the same sufferings we suffer. And our hope for you is firm, because we know that just as you share in our sufferings, so also you share in our comfort.
> (2 Corinthians 1:3–7)

What an honor it is to share, with someone who is going through trials, the great comfort with which God embraced me and that this person can be comforted by Him too.

If we hear from a person who has always had an easy life that

God takes care of us, we tend not to listen. If we hear it from someone who has gone through tough times, we tend to listen more carefully. Something they share with us will help. Often, people with great wisdom and understanding learned it from the trials and tribulations they went through.

A wise great-aunt of Randy's once said to me, "A guilty conscience is a good thing." I found it a rather strange statement at the time, but I have come to appreciate what she was saying. Our guilty consciences can save us from falling even further into our sinful nature.

Our natural tendency is not to be good but rather to enjoy living as we wish or doing things our way. We enjoy living in the moment. If it feels good, it must be good.

Our consequences and consciences are often what lead us to be in the hands of the Potter, God Himself. Allowing ourselves to become clay in the Potter's hand is the most awesome place to be.

The consequences of my abortion are truly what God used to show me who He was and how much I needed Him. This journey of dealing with the consequences of my abortion has taught me so much about life in general, and it has drawn me close to God.

When I discovered the blessings in the consequences of our sin, I could allow myself to continue to grow closer to my heavenly Father. Ultimately, God the Father came to me where I was and showed me that He loved me, regardless of my sin.

God used the consequences to get my attention and, ultimately, to draw me closer to Him, one step at a time. I realized that God was not out to get me or to get even; rather, it was to love me and claim me as His own child.

The biggest blessing that came from my abortion was that I came to know Jesus Christ as my Redeemer and Savior. There is nothing on earth more of a blessing than that.

Another blessing—after all the turmoil—is that my baby is in heaven with Jesus. Who can ask for anything better than that? The baby did die but is very much alive in Christ, right now and for always.

The guilt in my heart for my abortion was transformed to joy in my heart at what Jesus had done for me. I have a new song in my whole being that wants to sing out to the world about the freedom we can have from our abortions and other sins because of Jesus Christ. Some days, my heart is full to overflowing. What a blessing—and comfort!

We can claim the freedom to have free will, but nothing measures up to freedom in Christ.

> The sacrifices of God are a broken spirit; a broken and contrite heart, O God, you will not despise. (Psalm 51:17)

> He heals the broken-hearted and binds up their wounds. (Psalm 147:3)

Are we focused on the one who heals or the healing He has done?

> Now on his way to Jerusalem, Jesus traveled along the border between Samaria and Galilee. As he was going into a village, ten men who had leprosy met him. They stood at a distance and called out in a loud voice, "Jesus, Master, have pity on us!"
>
> When he saw them, he said, "Go, show yourselves to the priests." And as they went, they were cleansed. One of them, when he saw he was healed, came back, praising God in a loud voice. He threw himself at Jesus' feet and thanked him—and he was a Samaritan.
>
> Jesus asked, "Were not all ten cleansed? Where are the other nine? Was no one found to return and give praise to God except this foreigner?" Then he said to him, "Rise and go; your faith has made you well." (Luke 17:11–19)

That soul loved the Healer more than the healing and was made whole. How about you?

Alma's attention has gone to the Healer of both body and soul. That is how she can see blessings hidden in consequences. Other questions have arisen about her walk with God, and she has looked at them as they have come—but from the perspective that they were questions to help, not to hinder.

When and where do the consequences of your choice begin or end? Can it ever come to an end in this world or in the Christian world?

Perhaps not. Perhaps there is no end so we will not forget or diminish the significance of the event. There may be no limits to the consequences of our actions. Some actions bring results that cannot go away. Freedom is in Christ alone, not in time or space or any idea humans may come up with. Freedom is divine only.

I no longer want to forget what I did. Some of the consequences of our choices may be avoided by never sharing with anyone, but maybe there are consequences in being silent. One is that we may miss the help that is nearby for our spirits. Sometimes, helping someone else is more healing for us than for them.

I often look up to my heavenly Father to sustain me when I have days that trouble me. God is never far away and always is willing to give rest to weary souls, if only we ask.

As a friend of mine would say, "There are consequences for your choices." Life is all about choices! Is repentance truly cost-effective? Everything in life costs something, including true repentance.

The cost of not repenting is eternal damnation. What's a little repentance, compared to an eternity of suffering? Cost-effective? It's absolutely the best deal you'll ever get.

Why would any woman go through the pain of admitting what she has done wrong to God, only to be shunned by everyone around her, especially those in church?

Is there a double standard in our churches today? Is there a standard by which the "approved" members can lay heavier burdens on those whose sin is outside the norm or acceptable levels? Tragically, yes; the double standard thrives in our society and in our churches. Some churches heap heavy consequences on sinners whose fall was outside the church's authority.

Many can give testimony about treatment they received. Many more can witness to the treatment of others in this fashion. I have seen pregnant teens shunned and driven away from a church because of their mistake. This same thing can happen to alcoholics, prostitutes, drug addicts, murderers, homosexuals, thieves, adulterers, or sinners of any kind.

It's as though, once branded, you are not expected to change or turn out well. The people who do this to others give no hope. Some make comments like, "You can't teach an old dog new tricks," or "People don't change." If these ideas are true, then those people have no hope either because they will not change any more than the rest of us. If people don't or can't change, there is no hope for anyone.

These scenes are played out too often for my liking. There seems to be a prevailing attitude among some churchgoers that translates as, "This is church. You must be perfect. Sinners are not welcome."

We may not be able to change this attitude overnight, but we can approach the folks who have closed minds, one at a time, with a new outlook on sinners. Maybe these church folks will see that they too were sinners and need to be brought into the house of God. There is always hope for growth and acceptance. The Lord God can do wonderful works of grace in everyone who is willing to open themselves to Him.

I also must say that I have seen pregnant teens embraced by a church and guided to a better, holy life. People can and do change.

Which view does your church have—God's or the world's?

A worldview is that we should be forgiven on people's terms, not God's. Another worldview is that there should be values to different sins—a hierarchy of importance to them. Still another view is that we can run out of opportunities to be forgiven.

Some churches demonstrate their adherence to these views. There is a trend back to forgiveness, as Jesus asks. If there is repentance, we must forgive. There is no limit on size of sin, on frequency, or that any other person can adjust forgiveness. God's forgiveness is available to everyone who repents of their sin and asks forgiveness. We must do the same. We must extend the same.

The ultimate consequence for any sin is that we must answer to God. If we can answer now with, "I'm sorry; please forgive me," we will reap the ultimate blessing of forgiveness. Otherwise, we can answer later, on judgment day, with eternal damnation. Confessing our sin and asking forgiveness is something that begins at our conversion and continues throughout our lifetime on earth. Don't let up!

Jesus said, "But seek first his kingdom and his righteousness, and all these things will be given to you as well" (Matthew 6:33). Do that and reap God's blessings in the consequences of life.

We will not reap God's blessing without being in His kingdom first.

Another consequential blessing that I can clearly see is how much I have changed, with the help of my friend Jesus.

I can openly share my downfall and use it to witness to others. I can show God's grace and maybe lead them to the good news of God's grace for them and that He meets us where we are.

## LET GO AND LET GOD:

# TRUSTING CHOICE

Do you feel like you are always going two rungs up the ladder but falling back three? I struggled with that, and I got so tired of the ladder and trying to prove my own worth that I almost gave up. Thank God that He sustained me in those days. I learned to trust Him; you can too.

*Trust* means to rely on. We don't always rely on ourselves. If we don't rely on our own efforts or abilities, then we have to rely on someone else. Apply that to God, whom we cannot see, hear, feel, or smell. Trusting Him means taking one big step.

That big step is learning to trust someone other than ourselves, as well as trusting a God we must believe exists.

After years of trusting no one but ourselves, we become hardened to the world around us. The hardening is a shell of protection we construct with secrecy. Secrecy behind the shell feels comfortable and is at a level we can handle. To keep our secret, we trust no one but ourselves and perhaps a very few others.

The first step of trusting someone other than ourselves can be a complicated one. There are so many ways this could go. We can trust someone who is fully trustworthy, and we heal; or we can trust someone who is not trustworthy, and our secret becomes a weapon against us. There are myriad possibilities in between.

We must come to the place where we can risk putting our trust in someone else. That is a step toward putting our trust in God. Strangely and appropriately, where humans fail us, God does not.

One trustworthy friend is a blessing from God. When we find that friend who does not judge us and loves us as we are, it can be a great comfort. It must be someone with whom we can share, without fear of them telling others; someone who allows us to be totally transparent with them.

There is risk in trusting someone. Be careful, and find someone worth trusting, even if that person is not initially a friend or family member. Consider a counselor or the clergy.

Then we find out that God knew all along. Our secret is out.

I picture God as trustworthy now. He is the one who allows me to be completely open and transparent with Him. He loves unconditionally, as He always has, but I previously did not believe it. Remember that it pleases God to see us lean on His promises and have a desire to be closer to Him.

Can you trust that God has your best interest at heart? Can you trust that God has more power than people? Can you trust that what Satan means for evil, God can use for good?

In Genesis 50, we find the story coming to a close about Joseph and his faithfulness to God. In verse 20, we read about his reaction to his brothers' remorse over selling him as a slave in his youth. He declares his faith in God by his understanding of God's purposes in what had happened.

> "You intended to harm me, but God intended it for
> good to accomplish what is now being done, the
> saving of many lives." (Genesis 50:20)

We too can have this kind of faith. Trust in the Lord in all things.

After having my abortion, I did not trust my own judgment in the same way as before, so trusting God was not easy. Choosing to make an effort to trust God in the small things slowly built to trusting God in the big things.

> And we know that in all things God works for the
> good of those who love him, who have been called
> according to his purpose. For those God foreknew
> he also predestined to be conformed to the likeness
> of his Son, that he might be the firstborn among
> many brothers. And those he predestined, he also
> called; those he called, he also justified; those he
> justified, he also glorified. What, then, shall we
> say in response to this? If God is for us, who can be
> against us? (Romans 8:28–31)

If God can use all things for the good of those who love Him, then he can use our worst mistakes, as well as our best efforts. There are times when our worst mistakes are of more use to the Lord than our best efforts.

Take the time to ponder that thought. Personally, I have learned more from my mistakes than from the things I did right. The wisdom God gives is typically from practical training during our walks through life. Consider the pain in your life as a great gain in God's wisdom.

In our lowest moments, we can take comfort in knowing we are among friends. If they have been where we have been, we can trust them. If we trust them and they trust the Lord, then we too can trust the Lord—in time.

Finally, if we trust the Lord God Almighty, who better could we find? There is no other like Him in heaven or on earth.

Trusting God can be an issue. If we cannot trust ourselves, how do we learn to trust God and all He has to offer? We trusted ourselves before and made a wrong choice, so are we going to make another wrong choice? When we feel so overwhelmingly stupid and inadequate about a previous choice in life, we often doubt we can be trusted not to do it again.

So decision-making is definitely a problem. I still struggle in this area from time to time.

God is more trustworthy than we are. God is trustworthy! Amen to that. He does not make wrong choices. God does not change. If anyone has moved, it is us, not Him.

"If God is for us, who can be against us?" (Romans 8:31). Not even ourselves? Realize there is nothing we could do that would be sufficient to cover our sin. There is nothing of ourselves that would suffice in the sight of God to cover, if possible, our own sin. That's where God's grace is sufficient, not ours. We have to give up control of that too.

We are imperfect, and He requires a perfect sacrifice. We are incapable of it. We let ourselves down repeatedly in other areas too. Whenever we doubt ourselves, second-guess ourselves, or do not stand up for ourselves, according to our faith in God, we are, in a fashion, against ourselves.

Do trust and control go hand in hand?

Yes! At least, in some circumstances they can. We can desire control because we do not trust others with the control or because we simply want the control ourselves. To let others have control, we must trust to a degree.

The measurement of sin that I felt took place in my childhood left me feeling very defeated. I felt I could not reach the level of sinlessness required of me in church. I am realizing how many churches have a measure for sin.

Human understanding measures sin. Divine decree condemns it all. Divine love can forgive it all.

A pastor friend once said that we lose hundreds of people who backslide and never return to church. I'm certain that many of them are women who feel defeated, frustrated, and lonely. They are held up against the measuring stick of the people of the church and do not feel they measure up. They do not allow themselves to experience God's forgiveness and move into the joy of the Lord apart from the approval of other people.

This is one of the major reasons for this book—to show that not all those who place their faith in the Lord Jesus Christ are going to measure others that way. Some of us measure people by whether or not they choose to place their faith in Jesus. Some of us choose not to measure at all. We want you to know that Jesus paid for all of us, not just a select few. God's grace is extended to all who will come to Him for forgiveness. We should extend the same.

I believe that many of our churches today are desperately trying to protect their children from abortion and other social issues. I believe that if we did more than criticize or pass judgment on the abortion issue and, instead, opened it up for a loving and honest discussion, we would be ministering to both the women who have had abortions and our children. Education at any age helps us make better choices.

God's grace is sufficient to receive and should be sufficient to pass on to others.

God's grace is the same yesterday, today, and tomorrow. We need to give graciously to the women who need it. Most women who have had abortions will agree that there is a price to pay; that there are consequences, even though they may disagree as to what those consequences are. That is what our children need to hear—that there are consequences.

Our children need to hear there are consequences, and they need to hear there is grace. There are consequences to every sin, and there is grace sufficient for everything.

Our children also need to hear that abortion and other issues are addressed by God. Instead of saying abortion is wrong, perhaps we should tell them that abortion is not what God wants us to do. That would be sharing a truth, rather than passing a judgment. Saying that it's wrong is judging it; saying it's not God's will is sharing the truth of God's will for all of us.

Imagine what could be accomplished in our churches today if

we could love and respect one another, regardless of where we are or have been, what we have done or not done, and so on.

The views of the church can directly affect individuals' choices to continue to suppress their secret world—their "unforgivable" sin—or to be set free. Those church views did affect me. I chose to search in the Bible for God's truth and then admitted to myself and to Randy what I had done. Slowly, I realized God's truth would set me free, as He promised, if I trusted Him.

We can choose to live as if dangling in a birdcage that has the door wide open. I struggled with living within that sort of cage for a long time. I felt trapped with no way out. We can also choose to step out in faith and soar like eagles.

I felt that if I was open and honest about my abortion, I would face much rejection and hurt, both from my family and the church. I still fear there is some truth in this.

There was a certain level of comfort in staying in the cage. It was a safety net. If I chose to step out of that cage, there was a fear of falling; a fear that nothing would be there to catch me. Hanging on to the cage felt like my security.

This self-caging was in place of trusting that God would place something there for me to step onto to sustain me.

I dared to come out of the cage by trusting one promise of God at a time. The Bible is full of God's wonderful promises that we can trust.

Knowing our surroundings and staying in them seems easier than venturing into new territory. Familiarity is comfortable.

A lot of my fears were never realized. In general, being open and transparent about my abortion has been interesting. Church leaders have given me the pat answer about the "worst sin of abortion," which apparently was a standard answer set by the church. Family and acquaintances have been loving and understanding. Some acquaintances, however, gave me blank stares and no reaction.

The reaction I love to hear more than any other is, "I had one too." These women are opening a little. My complete joy will come when they find rest, peace, and joy in their life journeys with God.

With God's love, we can cast out our fears. The fears slowly flow out as God fills us with His truth, grace, and love. When we know we are loved by God, even while we were yet sinners, He gives us the strength to face our fears head-on. We can't fail with God on our side.

> There is no fear in love. But perfect love drives out
> fear, because fear has to do with punishment. The one
> who fears is not made perfect in love. (1 John 4:18)

Fear is an anxiety about a pending discomfort, such as punishment or judgment from others. As we are filled with God's love, there is no room for fear. We can cast out all fears, as they are no longer needed.

In the end, I was looking in Jesus's face as He set me free.

After working out my faith and learning to trust Jesus Christ, I understood John 8:31–32:

> To the Jews who had believed him, Jesus said, "If
> you hold to my teaching, you are really my disciples.
> Then you will know the truth, and the truth will set
> you free."

I also understood Numbers 32:23, which says, "Be sure your sin will find you out." I did choose to walk out of the cage and was fully blessed by God's forgiveness because I understood, trusted, and claimed His promises.

At some point in time and in our walk with the Lord, we must release our hold on our secrets and face the consequences. This is not to say the Lord will blab our stories around the community or the world, but we must allow Him to do as He sees best.

In order to grow spiritually, we must free everything about our lives to God. Even our strongest hold on something that we do not wish to relinquish must be given over to Him as a sacrifice. The fullest relationship with Him has no stronghold from Him.

Many songs relate to our giving all to Jesus. These were written by those who have given all to Him and who reaped the benefit of the freedom that comes from doing that.

Consider it repentance from self-control to God-control. In Matthew 3:2, John the Baptist declares, *"Repent, for the kingdom of heaven is near."* Give it all to God, and enter the fullness of a relationship with Him.

Am I holy because I am a pastor's wife? I don't think so! Am I holy because of what I have done? I don't think so! If I want Jesus to take the load of my sin, I also must want to give Jesus all the glory for anything good in me.

We are not in competition with anyone to become holy, but we act like we are. Becoming holy is a journey between God and us but no one else.

I tried for a long time to live a holy life, but my motives were wrong. I was trying to measure up by doing all the right things in order to be pleasing and forgiven by God. I never attained either of those because I was disappointing God. I didn't take God for who He says He is in the Bible. I tried to be holy on my own merits, but it can't be that way. God will not have it that way. He wants the credit for all of it. God requires us to become humble before Him, and He fills us and brings us to holiness.

I always questioned my life under self-control. Now, my life under God-control has been filled with His blessings and no more questions. I am under the peace of knowing that it is far easier to trust my life to my loving Father than it is to trust myself. I gave it all to God—the good, the bad, and the in-between.

Give more of yourself to God today than yesterday but less than you will tomorrow. When it is impossible to do this anymore, you likely will have reached the point of giving your all to Him. Start today.

# Transition 3

## Working Repentance:
### Repentance at Work

At the time of writing this book many statistical reports indicated that about 30 percent of women of childbearing age in North America have had an abortion. Different reports gave different results, but this seems to be the average. That's over one in four women. I find it interesting that women never tell me they had an abortion until I speak about mine first.

No one is talking about it. Can there be a full healing for us if we don't learn how to share with others who may be in the same situation? We behave as though there is nobody else who has made the same decision, even though the statistics prove differently.

Some people say we live in sinful times, as all people have. It began with Adam and Eve. God considered them to be sinners too.

We haven't managed to become better at this sin thing. I guess that's what makes the Bible just as alive and relevant today as it has been from the beginning. There never has been a time when the human race has needed the Word of God less or more than another time.

We must choose. We must repent. We must turn to the direction the Lord wants us to go and keep going in that direction. As we learn more, we need to turn more of our lives to that new direction and make gains—victory over sin, growth in integrity and spirit, and a strong witness for Jesus in our lives as His followers.

Repentance is a decision we must hold on to. It is a one-time decision and an everyday decision at the same time. We not only make this decision at one time in our lives to become Christians, but we must make it everyday to remain committed to following Christ and doing His will.

Repentance is an active experience and expression of sorrow and regret for sins.

A working repentance is a continual, concerted effort to become less like we were and more like we are supposed to be. A working repentance includes more aspects of a person each day, until the entire person is dedicated to serving the Lord.

Our aim, as Christians, should be to do as we are instructed in the Bible to do. That is to strive to become perfect, as our Savior is perfect. We know we will never fully attain that here on earth, but even our efforts can glorify God.

I dealt with guilt for twenty to twenty-five years for some of the sins I committed in my youth. I was overwhelmed with grief. I never decided to continue doing the things for which I felt sorry. Is that not repentance?

Yes! It is repentance. It is the beginning of repentance where one puts off the old self. A working repentance is where one starts and continues to put on the new self, the Christlike self.

> You were taught, with regard to your former way of life, to put off your old self, which is being corrupted by its deceitful desires; to be made new in the attitude of your minds; and to put on the new self, created to be like God in true righteousness and holiness. (Ephesians 4:22–24)

This is the ongoing effort to be all that we are called to

be—Christian. It is part of the overall process of regeneration in Christ.

There is a possibility of reaching full repentance. Even though there is always a chance we will decide otherwise, a fullness of repentance is possible when all our minds, bodies, and spirits are given over to the Lord. As I said, however, we can decide to take this back and lose the ground we have gained.

We are all sinners who can be saved by grace. Whose grace? You must know by now—God's! Matthew 5:48 encourages, "Be perfect, therefore, as your heavenly Father is perfect."

*Be perfect, as my heavenly Father is perfect? How can I ever accomplish that? Not in my wildest dreams or deepest desires; not with my abortion sin still in my life.* Have you thought something like that? It seems to be beyond what we can attain as Christians in this life. Let's see if we can make the connection between us and our perfect God and Savior. This may seem, at first, to contradict our way of thinking, but it doesn't contradict God's words or His ways.

It may seem confusing when we know we have sinned, and we can't find humans who are willing to forgive us, even in church. Never mind our ever daring to enter into God's presence and ask forgiveness—that would be ludicrous.

The confusion is because of a conflict of interests. The interests of the other people, even in church, are often self-seeking or self-satisfying, while the interest of God is for our salvation and our betterment. It boils down to a conflict between what people think and what God says.

But we can become perfect. The only catch is that it's not by our efforts but through the blood of Christ and His work at the cross.

Try this exercise to see if it helps you to better understand: Make a list of the sins and issues with which you struggle and have a fear of bringing to God; the things that keep you away from coming to God's throne. Picture in your imagination that you are passing that list to God. If you have accepted Christ as your Savior, God simply takes the list, tears it up, and throws it away because when He looks at you, He sees Jesus Christ, His Son. We are covered by the blood of Christ.

Now, here's the tricky part—and it took me years to get it. In time, I realized I was grieving the Holy Spirit and God by not believing God's Word and promises and by not trusting God to keep His Word and promises. When He says your sins are "as far as the east is from the west" (Psalm 103:12), He means it. It is His promise. He chooses to remember your sins no more, or at least He doesn't hold them against you. You can take Him at His word.

Please, do not let your mind wander from this path of thinking God loves you enough to help you. It is far too easy to follow a different path and end up thinking worse about yourself than you ought. God loves you and will not turn down an honest effort to come to Him with anything—and I do mean anything.

God's desire is for us to believe in Him, to praise Him, and to thank Him. We must also acknowledge that He keeps His promises. God deserves the glory for what Jesus has accomplished. What He accomplished was without any help from us.

We must be at work in our repentance. We must put an effort into turning our lives around from the old sinful ways to the new person in Christ Jesus. There must be progress of some sort in our lives, where we are changing or are in a change. It is by our choices that we change within ourselves, with the Lord's help.

If we have an honest desire to change, we can, with God's help. Often, our biggest change is in fully trusting in God's Word. Imagine that God has truly sent your sin as far as the east is from the west. You will realize they never meet. In other words, they are not there to condemn you. What an amazing change you should have within. Can you sense a new life within?

According to the definitions and passages given, repentance is a changing of the mind.

Do not conform any longer to the pattern of this world, but be transformed by the renewing of your mind. Then you will be able to test and approve what God's will is—his good, pleasing and perfect will. (Romans 12:2)

That is attitude. Our attitude shows the world where our hearts lie. It shows what we truly believe. If what we put our faith in is not of the Lord, then it will show. If our faith is moving from our own efforts to God, this too will show. This move in focus and faith is repentance working out salvation. This change in belief and trust and faith is repentance.

A caution—check the direction of repentance. It should be more and more toward the will of God. It should move in the direction Jesus walked in life.

Someone may well ask, "At what point could I consider myself upright enough to say 'It is done!'?" The answer will always be *never*—at least, not in this life. We may become fully repentant and fully devoted to the Lord God, but we will not become perfect, as our Jesus was perfect, until we meet Him. We must continually strive to be like Him.

We must be careful to not consider ourselves beyond improvement, even if we have no recognizable area to improve. That kind of thought can easily lead to pride, then arrogance, and, subsequently, sin. This slide is quick and deadly.

I believe you now have a good grasp of the chart on the next page. You probably have figured out where you are and where you are headed. Notice, though, that the little arrow at the bottom is pointing more toward God's will, which is righteousness. That arrow is pointing the direction you will be headed if you are at the place we are describing. You are headed in the right direction; keep working at it. Keep growing, keep improving, and keep following Jesus.

| The Process of Repentance | | | | |
|---|---|---|---|---|
| Sin | Remorse | Repentance | Working Repentance | Righteousness |
| our will | | | | God's will |
| absence of repentance | initial repentance | recognition of repentance | repentance at work | fullness of repentance |
| ← | \ | ↑ | / | → |
| Direction of focus | | | | |

# SECTION III

# BEYOND THE CROSS

STEPPING AWAY:

# CONTINUING CHOICE

I can virtually see myself getting off my knees at the cross and choosing to get to work for the Lord. With a thankful heart that is filled with His forgiveness and love, I have a desire to serve.

It is now time to move on in life. We can step away, beyond the cross, and grow in our sanctification in the Lord.

Everyone encounters a time when they must make a decision about what they believe. This time is called a *crisis moment*. The crisis is the time when a decision must be made; it can be delayed no longer.

There are several of these crisis moments in life. They include the good times, like the moment when you decide to marry that someone special or that moment when you accept that you are about to become a parent and prepare yourself for the responsibilities that accompany it. They also include the harder times of life, when we must decide to continue in the face of uncertainty or undesirable circumstances. Facing the looming death of an ill loved one is an example of this kind of crisis moment.

The crisis moment we speak of here is the fuller decision to follow Christ. Sometimes, this is manifested in a dedication to full-time service or simply a more consistent devotion to study and growth in our relationship with God.

> In my Father's house are many rooms; if it were not so, I would have told you. I am going there to prepare a place for you. (John 14:2)

God has prepared a place, a mansion, for us in heaven—for us undeserving sinners, repentant sinners, people willing to admit we are wrong. We have done something against Him, and what does He do for us? He prepares a place in a mansion for us. A mansion in heaven made out of rubies, sapphires, diamonds, precious gold, and other gems—all for us. We are more precious to God than the mansions He prepares. And He wants fellowship with us more than those mansions. That is amazing love. Who could fathom, who could take this in, and not be overwhelmed by God's grace? It is no longer what I have done but rather who He is.

God gave me a new heart, one that could love myself once again and love others in return, as a servant of Christ. I have learned and allowed myself to love myself again and not to look at myself with disgust. I can look in the mirror and love what I see. I am who I am, and all that I am is only because of Christ. I thank God for blessing me with my husband, who always freely extends God's grace to me.

No matter how deep your hurt is, God can go even deeper and mend your heart.

It is not possible for us to look at others with love if we cannot look at ourselves that way. When Christ told us to love others as we love ourselves—"And the second is like it: 'Love your neighbor as yourself'" (Matthew 22:39)—He was also telling us to love ourselves.

When we look at ourselves in the mirror, the reflection is sometimes distorted. How can we love that which seems distorted to us? How can we love that which we do not understand? How can we love that which is foreign to us?

God can give us back the ability to love as He has directed us. He can give us love that we may convert to love for ourselves and others. *"Everything is possible for him who believes"* (Mark 9:23). God can unwarp the mirror.

You will never live a victorious life or move ahead in any way with God if you stay in bondage.

Bondage is to old and wrong beliefs, old and wrong ways of doing things, and old and wrong ideas of what is right or wrong.

The old belief was that we were not worth the sacrifice Jesus made. The old way of doing things was in our own strength and power, not God's. And the old ideas of right and wrong were based on what the world said, not what God says. They were wrong.

We must grow; there is no standing still. Life goes on whether we believe it or not. There is no going back to redo life either. We must grow spiritually, and the only effective growth is for eternity in the Lord Jesus.

Step away from the ties that bind and be free in Christ. Then, be productive.

God can use us before we allow His transforming power to touch us but not to our fullest capacity. I know women who serve God in tremendous ways, but they are still in bondage because they have not found freedom from their issues, abortion or otherwise. I would love to see them once they have allowed God to touch this area of their lives and do a work in them. What potential we all have in Christ.

Once this has been put in its proper place, you become a clean vessel, which God has the power to do, and you can become a beacon of light to others around you, like you can't even imagine. God is great, and that's the point—God is great. He is great enough to make you a clean vessel and great enough to make you a beacon of light, if you choose to allow Him.

We cannot lead anyone any farther than we have been ourselves. How can we effectively convince others that God's grace exists if we don't believe it to its limit of fulfilling victorious power?

Satan uses many worldly things, good and bad, to keep us occupied so we don't do what God calls us to do or to hinder what we are attempting to do. We must remember and rely on Philippians 4:10–13, which says,

> I rejoice greatly in the Lord that at last you have renewed your concern for me. Indeed, you have been concerned, but you had no opportunity to show it. I am not saying this because I am in need, for I have learned to be content whatever the circumstances.

I know what it is to be in need, and I know what it is to have plenty. I have learned the secret of being content in any and every situation, whether well fed or hungry, whether living in plenty or in want. I can do everything through him who gives me strength.

In 2 Corinthians 12:7–10, the apostle Paul cautions us,

To keep me from becoming conceited because of these surpassingly great revelations, there was given me a thorn in my flesh, a messenger of Satan, to torment me. Three times I pleaded with the Lord to take it away from me. But he said to me, "My grace is sufficient for you, for my power is made perfect in weakness." Therefore I will boast all the more gladly about my weaknesses, so that Christ's power may rest on me. That is why, for Christ's sake, I delight in weaknesses, in insults, in hardships, in persecutions, in difficulties. For when I am weak, then I am strong.

## Grace: A Walk with Paul

On the road to Damascus (Acts 9), Paul was transformed by God's touch and by God's grace. He definitely became a new creation in Christ. Amazingly, Paul found God's grace sufficient (2 Corinthians 12:9), and he allowed God's grace to cover all his past. The Christians he had persecuted before he was claimed as one of God's own were still a part of his past. Accepting that God's grace is sufficient to cover Paul's past seems somehow easier than trusting God can do the same for us. Why do we feel we are so much worse than anyone else?

Paul's trust in God's Word must have been uplifting because he continued to serve God in wonderful ways. That's what God wants from us. Believing and trusting that God's grace is sufficient is, in fact, obeying God and showing our love for Him.

When Paul was in prison, he could rejoice in the Lord because he remembered his own past. I wonder whether Paul's "thorn in the flesh" (2 Corinthians 12:7) was all the memories of his past. Regardless, he could sing to the Lord and be content while in prison because he was very much aware of where he came from and how God's touch changed him. Paul's desires revolved around serving his Master in the best way he could, no matter where he was.

Paul did not beat himself up about where he had been. Instead, he learned to look at where he was going—eternity with God.

We only encumber our lives, to the point of almost being useless to God, when we continue to focus our attention on things of the past. When we set our eyes on things above, then and only then can God help us soar.

Even though Paul considered himself to be least of the apostles (1 Corinthians 15:9–10) and less than the least of all God's people (Ephesians 3:7–9), he became a great tool used by God to proclaim the good news. Paul had allowed God to be the Potter and him to be the clay, used as God had directed him.

Paul's attention was on things above and his work for the Lord. We can do likewise and join with Paul in his praises to God.

Paul's thorn in the flesh—could it be guilt and shame within himself for having persecuted and killed Christians before his conversion at Damascus? Did the faces of the people he killed ever leave his mind? He could not turn the clock back and redeem life, nor could he change or erase what he had done.

Somehow, Paul had to deal with his life. I think that the only way he could do that was to lay it down at the foot of the cross. I am sure that faces, reactions, certain moments, and incidents must have stuck in his memory. Only by God's grace could he continue on. Continuing on was to serve the Lord, Master, Savior who could give him refuge from what he was guilty of. Paul was a prisoner at times, but he was fully saved by grace and in God's mercy.

Do we continue to live in a prison we have created, which we allow Satan to use against us?

Do we take pleasure in our weaknesses and allow the power of Jesus to shine through? Do we accept the thorns we have as gifts from God to show His grace through us? Have we made ourselves nothing, that He may be everything to us?

> For it is by grace you have been saved, through faith—and this not from yourselves, it is the gift of God. (Ephesians 2:8)

> But he said to me, "My grace is sufficient for you, for my power is made perfect in weakness." Therefore I will boast all the more gladly about my weaknesses, so that Christ's power may rest on me. (2 Corinthians 12:9)

Sufficient enough to set me free; free to soar on wings like eagles! What can I say but hallelujah to that!

Choose this day to completely surrender to God's will. Receive His promises, love, and grace. And may you too be able to shout *hallelujah* with a joyful heart.

Leave the past where it is, and press on toward the mark that the Lord has laid before you, the mark of perfection in Christ.

> I press on toward the goal to win the prize for which God has called me heavenward in Christ Jesus. (Philippians 3:14)

It is in He who saves that we find our worth, our purpose, and our calling in this life and the next.

Never underestimate the purpose God has for you.

ABUNDANT LIFE:

# FREEDOM CHOICE

When we think of abundant life, what crosses our minds? Could it be financial success to meet our every want; or robust health so we don't have to worry about illness or becoming a celebrity or member of royalty so we could be popular? There are as many possibilities as there are people in the world.

God meets us in all those ways but not always in the way we might expect.

God's concern for our finances or financial success is likely more in our willingness to sacrifice than our desire to gain. His concern for our health is likely for our spiritual health and eternal life, rather than a fit body here and now. Being popular with Him and being a princess or prince in His kingdom are more important to Him than having that here on earth.

Is this easy? Not always. We benefit sometimes, but God notices when we put others before ourselves. That is truly abundant life. I've discovered that excuses do not carry any weight with God when we neglect our duty to Him to do as He asks.

*Abundant life is when:*

> You no longer depend on your goodness but rest instead on Jesus Christ.
>
> You soar like an eagle because you are no longer weighed down with guilt and shame, so you are free to fly.

You look to God for direction on where to go next in life.

You can look in the mirror and no longer need to run away from what you see; you can see the new creation in Jesus Christ, our Lord; you've traded in the crimson rags to become white as snow.

You can go to bed at night, having replaced some of the anxiety with peace of mind.

Abundant life also is freedom in Christ.

But thanks be to God that, though you used to be slaves to sin, you wholeheartedly obeyed the form of teaching to which you were entrusted. You have been set free from sin and have become slaves to righteousness.

I put this in human terms because you are weak in your natural selves. Just as you used to offer the parts of your body in slavery to impurity and to ever-increasing wickedness, so now offer them in slavery to righteousness leading to holiness. When you were slaves to sin, you were free from the control of righteousness. (Romans 6:17–20)

It's everlasting.

For God so loved the world that he gave his one and only Son, that whoever believes in him shall not perish but have eternal life. (John 3:16)

It's full.

But the fruit of the Spirit is love, joy, peace, patience, kindness, goodness, faithfulness, gentleness and self-control. Against such things there is no law. (Galatians 5:22–23)

It's abundant life.

> For everyone who has will be given more, and
> he will have an abundance. Whoever does not
> have, even what he has will be taken from him.
> (Matthew 25:29)

Even if it's only two days long, life can only be abundant because
we have the Holy Spirit in us, Christ beside us, and God the Father
before us.

*Abundance* refers to a plentiful supply, more than enough, or
fully sufficient. There is more than enough mercy, love, and grace
from God available to each of us. That is abundant life!

What is abundant life to you? Is it quantity, quality, or both? Is it
material, spiritual, or relational or maybe a combination? Is abundant
life what happens to us, in us, or from us? Consider it a while.

Recently, Randy and I went to a flea market at a small church, and
I bought a pendant for fifty cents. When I picked it up, I mentioned
to Randy that I was certain it was diamonds surrounding a ruby. I
couldn't tell for certain because it had no shine to it; it was really
dirty. I decided to take it home and clean it up.

Before I cleaned it, I asked a friend what she thought, and she
said, "It has no shine, and diamonds shine." What truth!

I cleaned it up later and discovered that it was, in fact, diamonds—
with a lot of shining power once the dirt was removed.

We are much like those diamonds. Satan tries to keep us at the
same place as those dirty diamonds so we will not shine for God.
But we are precious diamonds to God, and He wants us to shine and
be a light to the world.

Some of us know we are saved by the blood of Christ, but Satan
tries to make sure we don't shine for Christ by telling us lies, which
we often believe. We must choose not to believe the lies, though.
Otherwise, we can easily think God must be disappointed with us.
We wonder if He has died for us, just to have us keep His truth to

ourselves. If we take Satan's lies as truth, then we take God's truth as lies. How confused we can be.

In fact, Jesus died so we could have eternal life and abundant life here on earth, as long as we live.

Again, that warped mirror shows its face. Again, we must unwarp the mirror and see things as they truly are. We must see the real truth, not the lies. We must remember our allegiance to God.

> I am not ashamed of the gospel, because it is the power of God for the salvation of everyone who believes: first for the Jew, then for the Gentile. (Romans 1:16)

That particular verse has been repeating in my heart and head. I sense that, in an awkward sort of way, by not claiming the abundant life for which Jesus died, I am ashamed of the gospel of Christ.

Believing in God's promises proves we are not ashamed of the gospel or ashamed of who He is and what He has done, as we must not be if we want Jesus to not be ashamed of us. Our pride must come down to this before we are blessed with abundant life, which only comes from being in God's will.

When Joshua walked around Jericho (Joshua 6), he had to do things that seemed foolish to some so that God could get the glory. We too, at times, must do things that seem foolish to some so that God will get the glory.

We can become the light of God and be a great beam of light for Him by believing the gospel first. It can set us free—free indeed—by sharing the gospel with others

If the truth will set us free (John 8:32), then the truth given to others may set them free. That is a great reason to share the truth with them.

I found out that God's grace, His free gift of love, was great enough to cover my sins. I am always struck that even though I can place myself at the cross two thousand years ago and help to hammer in the nails, His grace is more beautiful with each passing day. (By the way, take notice that the size of the nail is always the same, regardless of the sin.)

He outstretched His arms, side to side, and said, *I love you this much*, and then died for me. I have joy in the Lord. He has given me wings to soar like an eagle. He has covered me with His blood. He has looked ahead in time and called me by my name. He has loved me just as I am, loved me unconditionally, and blessed me with a husband who is an example of what true unconditional love is.

There is so much more to life than our pasts. There is also the present and the future. And even though there is not much we can do about the future, other than our best now, the present is not as bad as we may think it is.

> Therefore do not worry about tomorrow, for tomorrow will worry about itself. Each day has enough trouble of its own. (Matthew 6:34)

Look after today and today alone. If you look after it properly, tomorrow will be just fine, no matter what happens.

Life is held only today and is available to all those who are participating. Don't live anywhere else. Live here, while you can. The present is a present from God to you.

You've heard the saying, "Diamonds are a girl's best friend." Well, repentant sinners are God's diamonds. Give yours back to Him.

That crazy warped mirror has been flattened out, and now the mirror shows the truth. Much beauty is shown in that mirror. Enjoy the view. Enjoy what God's smooth mirror is showing you about who you are to Him and in Him.

If you have given your repentant heart to the Lord, you can live free in Him. Remain in Him, and enjoy that freedom in its fullest.

You have much to catch up on; the lost years spent in pain and fear are behind you. The found years of joy, peace, and love in Christ are ahead of you, starting now. Make them the best years by far. Make the most of them that you can as you walk with your Creator. Stay close to Him, and they will be wonderful years, even if they are not all pleasant.

If you focus on the mirror now, you will find you are no longer alone. Christ is with you, and His beauty that shines brightly also shines brightly through you. The cross of Christ is close and has replaced the pain of the abortion (or whatever your issue was) with thankfulness for what He accomplished for you on the cross. You might find yourself asking, "What can I do for You, Lord, in return for what You did for me so I could have eternal life?"

How did I get here? I kept moving. Sometimes it felt like backward movement, but it was slowly forward for the Lord.

If God is working in you, and you feel His grace, you have to do something about it. You can't be satisfied with the status quo or standing still any longer. God keeps working on you as long as you are willing to move to something more, something new. He helps you see things from different angles, ones you didn't even know were there.

It's like the surprise behind door number three. Door number one holds the lies Satan wants you to believe; the ones that say you are not worth saving. Behind door number two is a life lived on a day-to-day basis, hoping you've worked out your worth by those endless, resented, and tiresome efforts to save yourself. Door number three contains a full-length mirror that you are set free to look in and see yourself for who really you are; it's the one that shows you don't need to run away anymore or turn away from your Creator, God. You know that you know (that you know) that God sees all, knows all, and can forgive all. And you know God loves you, regardless of your past, your sins, or anything else. Sin, past or recent, can no longer have a hold on you because God sees you as His child.

The Bible says, "By grace you are saved … so that no one can boast … For we are God's workmanship, created in Christ Jesus" (Ephesians 2:8–10). In Christ Jesus, you are free to be something more—perfect in Jesus, holy, sanctified, and where God leads you. What an abundant life that is. God's family picture is *big*!

## WHAT OTHERS SEE:

# INTEGRITY CHOICE

I was raised to maintain honesty and integrity as a high standard. Living with my secret was very difficult, and it complicated my life very much because I could no longer maintain honesty and integrity. It was difficult to look in the mirror and not feel like a hypocrite.

The difficulties had a lot to do with my coming to see the true person I was staring at in the mirror. I was fully aware that while I was looking in the mirror, there was a whole lot more to the person I was looking at than the exterior I was facing.

We all can add the inner person to the shell we gaze at in the mirror. Even if others cannot see the inner person, we can. Occasionally, a spouse or close friend begins to see the inner person as well but only what we allow them to see.

There comes a point when hiding from God is no longer an option either. It is no longer appropriate to lie or pretend anything other than the truth. This is the point where integrity truly comes into play.

Integrity is when the truth is so much a part of you that there is no other option. Integrity is having every part of you testify that you are a Christian. Anything you stand for or do, outside of being like Christ, shows a lack of integrity. And believe me; others see it. They see the truth about you, whether you think they do or not. They may not know what you did, but they will know you did something.

I was a carpenter for many years and had the opportunity to enter hundreds of homes. After a while, I realized that people often put up facades, or false fronts, so I would not see the real them.

It became obvious because they could not keep up the show for extended periods. Very few can; none should.

If I was working in the home for only a day or two, they could lead me to believe they were a pretty good family. If I were working there for a week or more, the outcome was different. By the end of a full week, the truth would come out. They could not keep up the facade any longer than that; at least, none have yet.

Granted, the tendency in our society is to try to look good. Almost all of us succumb to this attitude to some degree. None of us is perfect, even though we want others to think we are.

We can have great peace of mind and can sleep well at night if we don't put on airs or try to be what we are not. This is possible; I have seen it.

Occasionally, I would work in a home where there was no difference at the end of a week, two weeks, or any amount of time. This was because these people were truthful about themselves from beginning to end. They were who they seemed to be, warts and all. They had integrity in their lives. We all need this kind of integrity.

God sees through us from the beginning. There is no possibility of fooling Him. Why not have integrity in our lives so we don't have to fool each other?

A wise person once said to me that the church aborts women who have had abortions. Someone also said that we seem to draw the people to church, but then we lose them. I know where some are and why they chose to leave. They come looking for the forgiveness Jesus offers, and they might find that, but do we give it to them? Do we give them unconditional love in the way Jesus gives—freely? Maybe not always. I hope that Jesus is so much a part of me that they can sense my nonjudgmental attitude. I am not appointed by God to judge anyone.

Our integrity should demand that we are the same today as we were yesterday and will be tomorrow. Our integrity demands that we love and accept as Christ did and taught us. Our integrity demands that if we are not there, we must head in that direction.

Now we see but a poor reflection as in a mirror;
then we shall see face to face. Now I know in part;
then I shall know fully, even as I am fully known.
(1 Corinthians 13:12)

When you go from not liking what you see in the mirror to loving who you have become because of Christ, you can claim to be a new creation and a miracle. We need to realize that we cannot believe in God's Word and Satan's lies at the same time and draw closer to God.

At our church family camp, some friends of ours commented that I had changed. They shared that I appeared bolder and had come out of my shell. I wonder why they would have seen me that way. Maybe Christ had much to do with it (Acts 4:29). I believe that what they see now is true only because of the freedom I have found in Christ Jesus.

The boldness anyone sees must be from God because I was a very shy person. The boldness is because of the mission my heavenly Father has entrusted to me to reach some of the hurting women in our world who are desperately looking for His grace.

When you feel free to look at yourself in the mirror and face up to all that you are, all that you have been, and all that you can become through God, you are at liberty to let others see you for all you are. Your mirror reflects the image of Christ and that you are a child of God, a new creation. Tell me: what's not to love about that?

God knows everything about me, and I have no need to try to hide from Him anymore. He has walked alongside me and helped me unwarp my mirror. His image of me—or you—was never warped.

Being open and honest with myself led to being open and honest with God and now with others.

I pray that what others see is more of Christ and less of me.

Let this be a daily prayer and objective!

What a difficult chapter this was to write. Maybe it should be called "What We Hope Others See." We all have hopes for what others see, but we also have fears of what they see.

Every once in a while, fear plays a part in my life. I realize that fear is not from God, but in my humanity, I do fail from time to time.

Overcoming fear regarding my writing this book has been a journey in itself, but I have attempted to follow God's leading and learn to trust Him and not myself.

I have run up against a few roadblocks regarding my abortion and this book, and God used each one to teach me, strengthen me, and bring me out of the fear. He brought me to be more concerned with what He asked of me than with the reaction of humankind.

RESPONSIBILITY:

# RESPONSIBILITY CHOICE

My journey with my heavenly Father throughout these years has been very much like a parent/child relationship. I've often looked at my own children to assess how my heavenly Father might have looked at me, His child.

I know now that He is patient, kind, loving, merciful, faithful, and so on, much more than I could ever imagine. I also know there were days when God was chuckling at me.

I am certain there was much intercession for me and the direction I would choose to go with different matters. I am certain He shook His head at some of my choices, but my heart sincerely attempted to please Him. All in all, God knows my heart above all, and He knows who I am choosing to serve, whether myself or Him.

The God of truth, who has freed us through our repentance and His mercy and grace, has given us the right to sit with Him on His throne in heaven (Revelation 3:14–22). He requires more than that we gain for ourselves; He also requires that we give of ourselves. We must give freely. God wants from us a desire to become more like His Son, Jesus Christ. God does not want us to be only lukewarm. He would like for us to become holy and perfect, like His Son, Jesus Christ (Romans 12:1–2).

I could not comprehend how I could ever become holy and perfect when I'd done such an awful act, but it is our responsibility to make every effort to move toward that goal of being holy and perfect, as Christ is.

> I press on toward the goal to win the prize for which God has called me heavenward in Christ Jesus. (Philippians 3:14)

Just as we do not want to take responsibility for our actions during crisis, we do not want to take responsibility for living a holy life, fully dedicated to God.

Nothing pleases me more or gives me more satisfaction than to know I am completely in God's will. There is a peace and a rest unlike any other in that place. There is a satisfaction in my senses more pleasing than any other accomplishment in this life.

I fought in life to maintain what I considered a reasonable lifestyle for my family. Work dried up, businesses closed, and people moved away, putting me out of work. I received bad news at times, when things should have looked good. I worked diligently at jobs I did not want but needed to support my family. All the while, I was not satisfied with my life.

When I was forty-five, after many years trying to figure out what to do, Alma offered to support me while I retrained to do whatever I felt would satisfy me. After a year of prayer, thought, and soul-searching to discover that satisfaction, I had no answers.

At forty-six, discouraged and downcast, Alma asked if I might want to become a pastor. Within two days of that suggestion, I knew it was where I needed to be.

Today, as I stand in the pulpit and declare the good news of Jesus Christ, I know without a doubt that I am where I need to be. This is the happiest I can imagine being, even with the challenges and difficulties of the job.

Taking on our responsibilities for the Lord is the most satisfying thing we can do. It ends our hunger. It finishes our purposes in life.

It is not by receiving but by giving.

Do we still fail? Yes, we do at times, but God knows the desires of our hearts and sees our pure motives. He is a patient God. As we found out with our children, nothing is learned over night, either as a parent or a child. While God has nothing to learn, we do, and He is patient with us.

Warm up to the idea of being responsible. Don't neglect looking in the mirror and checking out yourself. Completely open yourself to hear God's voice and His direction for your life.

He has plans for you.

> "For I know the plans I have for you," declares the LORD, "plans to prosper you and not to harm you, plans to give you hope and a future. Then you will call upon me and come and pray to me, and I will listen to you. You will seek me and find me when you seek me with all your heart." (Jeremiah 29:11–13)

Trust Him and become "hot" for serving Him. Becoming hot for the things of God shows Him our appreciation for what Jesus has done. This is by desiring to be more like our Savior. This also gives us peace of mind. It truly is a win/win situation.

First Samuel 15:22 reads, "Obedience is far better than sacrifice." In other words, God desires that we are obedient; it pleases Him. We need to check ourselves frequently as to whether we are being obedient in our relationship with our heavenly Father.

Obedience may not always be your first choice, but it will be the best choice. Usually, that's where you are the most content and rewarded. Obedience is a sure sign of listening to God and what He wants, not you.

In obedience, we learn another lesson from God, and that is trust. The two go hand in hand. As we learn to trust God, our obedience becomes a more natural response to Him.

My sincere thankfulness for what Jesus has done for me in all its capacity left me yearning to serve Him. This also left me with another choice—to be responsible with my life and live my life in a way that glorifies God, or to take His forgiveness and run off on my own.

Choosing to live a lukewarm life can be very dangerous and often leads to disappointment. We tend to desire to live in our sinful nature, but we can overcome that with God's help. Our obedience to the ways of God is the right step in the right direction to a more fulfilling life with the Lord.

Please remember that we must periodically check ourselves to make sure we are not, once again, getting into a works-for-salvation mode but are doing things purely so God will get the glory. Sometimes, it's hard to see this clearly, but with time, God will help us to see who actually is getting the glory.

I have heard it said that the responsibility of one who has been saved is to reach back and help someone else along. We not only need to reach forward to God but backward to the lost and hurting whom we once were among.

Randy and I gladly take on that responsibility. We hope that reaching out to you with this book has been helpful to you.

Now, it's your turn to reach back.

## SHARING WITH OTHERS:
# CHARITY CHOICE

A friend shared with me the same thought that I'd had: "I want to shout it from the rooftop." I assume it might have something to do with wanting to comfort others in the way Christ has comforted us, as 2 Corinthians1:4 encourages us: "[God] who comforts us in all our troubles, so that we can comfort those in any trouble with the comfort we ourselves have received from God."

Again, Luke 12:48 explains:

> But the one who does not know and does things deserving punishment will be beaten with few blows. From everyone who has been given much, much will be demanded; and from the one who has been entrusted with much, much more will be asked.

Simply put, where much is given, much is expected.

In order to have a desire to share with others, we who believe must have been touched by God's grace. He is my driving force, and it is only to honor and glorify Him that I do this.

God's abounding love and grace toward me leaves me feeling greatly indebted to Him. I have a deep desire to serve Him in any way I can, to show God my gratitude for making me an heir of His kingdom.

The comforts and encouragements I have had to carry me through this—the experience, the redemption, and the growth—is from my Lord. I only wish I could help impart that comfort to His other beloved children—namely, you.

My being willing to open up to my past has often left it open for others to share their stories. Sometimes, it's the same story; sometimes, it's not. I have been amazed that when we try to be perfect, we don't score too high with others. When we put our guards down and allow people to see us for who we are, life is much easier, perhaps because we no longer live a life of pretense. Real people like real people.

Are we not called to help others carry their burdens—not to take burdens from them but simply to help?

> Carry each other's burdens, and in this way you will
> fulfill the law of Christ. (Galatians 6:2)

A burden is a heavy load, one that is more than the usual life situation. These are the events and decisions we make that bring calamity and heartache in the deepest sense. They include but are not limited to abortion, rape, abuse, divorce, murder, and so on—the traumas of life. We need help with these kinds of burdens. We need to help with these kinds of burdens.

By sharing, we tell others that they are not alone. If they can realize this, even if no one talks about it, they can take comfort. God loves, regardless.

Satan loves to deceive us, and he instills fear in us. One of our fears may be that we are not knowledgeable enough in the Bible to share with others. God can use our testimonies, even in their simplest form, to heal us and to encourage others. Usually, when we are willing to encourage others, we, in turn, are encouraged.

Years ago, I taught a Sunday school class of young children. A girl in my group wanted to know how we could be certain that God forgave our sins. Her question forced me to come up with answers that, in turn, encouraged me—maybe even more than it encouraged her. God always amazes me that He works to get to our minds and our hearts.

Randy and I have heard, "A private sin requires a private confession, and a public sin requires a public confession." I have confessed, as I have needed to do. Now, I share so others may find freedom in the Lord Jesus Christ. I am not confessing now; I am sharing. There's a difference.

Sometimes, a private sin needs to be made public to help others. Sometimes it doesn't. Achan (Joshua 7) was punished publicly for something only he and the Lord knew about. It affected all of Israel, though; that is why there was a public confession and punishment.

What God requires of us—and the only thing we can do—is to administer His grace to others in the same manner we receive it from God. If we can extend only a small amount of grace to others, it may be because we have received or needed to receive only a small amount from God. There is an unlimited amount available, so the restriction would be ours.

> Therefore, there is now no condemnation for those who are in Christ Jesus, because through Christ Jesus the law of the Spirit of life set me free from the law of sin and death. (Romans 8:1–2)

If we are left with no condemnation and are free, how much more could we desire to have before the love and grace God has bestowed on us comes oozing out of us toward others? Should we not be left with a deep-rooted thankfulness for God's grace that drives us to the point of shouting from the rooftop? Even that desire is from God Himself.

> Being confident of this, that he who began a good work in you will carry it on to completion until the day of Christ Jesus. (Philippians 1:6)

The God who has begun His work in you will not easily let go of you. Just listen to His small voice, and you will be shouting from the rooftop too.

Sharing with others does not mean we must tell all the sordid details of our miserable lives. Our God wants us to share *Him*. We are asked to share our relationship, our salvation, and our stories with those around us so they too may come to know the Lord.

Whether we call it sharing, witnessing, or giving testimony, the idea is to tell others about what God has done for us.

Because many don't know what is expected when sharing, here is an example: Answer the five W's (who, what, when, where, why) and the one H (how).

Who are you, and who is God, in your words? Who were you before salvation, and who are you now?

What were you like before you began your relationship with God? What happened to change that?

When did it happen (not just the date, but when in your life; at what stage of your belief)?

Where have you been affected by the Lord—what areas of your life, specifically?

Why did you decide to change?

Why are you telling others now?

Why should others change or repent?

How did you change (what is different)?

How can others accept the Lord Jesus Christ as their Savior?

Do you need to tell them that you had an abortion or anything else? No! That is not necessary. We all can admit we are sinners, but we don't need to tell what the sin is to just anyone. Our sins were against the Lord and those against whom we sinned. Only they need our confession and repentance.

At some point, we no longer desire to see our own reflections in the mirror, but we should be the reflection of Christ for others. This would be truly sharing our Lord with those who need Him.

I have a vision of God's hand sweeping through our nation like a gentle wave of the sea. I can picture Him blessing our land as we come before Him in true repentance.

We should become mirror images of our Lord and Savior. We should become reflections of His love and grace toward others. Now, we no longer are looking for ourselves in the mirror but rather to be a reflection of Christ to others.

Shouting from the rooftop now comes easily.

## SERVING OTHERS:

# CHRIST'S CHOICE

The best example of servanthood is our Lord and Savior, Jesus Christ. He was willing to die on the cross so we could become His sisters and brothers and share His inheritance with Him.

As servants, our attitude toward others should reflect Jesus Christ when we do things for them, having their best interest at heart. This does not mean giving them everything they want, and they may not want what is good for them.

We usually want things that are for our personal pleasure, not the greater good, but getting our way could be what got us in trouble in the first place.

There are times in our lives when we could bail someone out of their crisis or distress, but God calls us to just walk beside them and share the burden. God cannot teach others if we always aim to make life easy for them by relieving them of their burdens. Our learning when to intervene or not intervene takes time and a lot of prayer.

Most of the beneficial things I learned in life came through tough times. I now understand that it's easier to step aside and watch God work than to try to do it myself. God usually has a purpose for everything in our lives, good or bad. God can use everything for good.

I originally thought my cause for writing this book was to reach out to women who had had an abortion, but my cause is to be a servant of God. He died for me on the cross, so how could I be anything less? My burden is to do as He has stirred my spirit to do and to give Him all the glory and honor in the process.

We make mistakes and fall into the dirt. Christ brings us out of the mire. It is not by anything we have done that we are saved but by the gift of God to us. He asks us to serve each other in love.

Our greatest service toward another is leading that person toward Christ. The Bible tells us that we can get a crown of glory for our service to Jesus, but I plan to give mine to Him for what He has done for me. How about you?

Our servant attitude, I believe, is a direct indication of our becoming holy. Being holy is not about what we look like but what Jesus looks like to others through us. Being holy is being set apart from the world for the service of God.

In holiness, we focus less on ourselves and more on God and others and how we can serve others. It's definitely not for personal gain but for the glorification of God. I struggled with this for many years, and when I finally took God and His Word for truth, my focus changed from myself to others. I gradually learned to love myself and my reflection in the mirror, as well as others more, as God's Word became alive in my being, soul, and mind. I also began to see Christ in the mirror more, rather than myself.

True repentance is an awesome process before our God. Jesus Christ walks beside us all the way, just like a brother. We too can walk beside our brothers and sisters, as Christ did.

When we let go of our guilt and shame, it's like allowing God's purifying love to come into the crevices of our minds, hearts, beings and, ultimately, our souls, allowing His healing power to mend our brokenness. We allow Him His right to bestow His grace upon us until we overflow with thanksgiving to Him; then others. That overflowing can be expressed by our service to others.

As long as we choose to remain in our mindsets of not allowing His grace to cover our sin, God cannot use us to our full potential. If we choose not to allow God to forgive us completely, we are choosing to continue to look at ourselves and others with our own measuring stick of what we have done wrong. We can choose to let go and find ourselves looking at ourselves and others differently. Instead of looking at others in condemnation, we will find ourselves extending God's unconditional love and forgiveness. (There are times I can sense God's love overflowing from me, and that is not of myself but of God.) We can see others, not for who they are but for what they can become with God's love and grace.

I don't consider myself a writer, but God is, and if He chooses to inspire someone like me to write something, then He can give the words. He also can use the words to heal someone else. The Bible was God-inspired. I wonder if those writers were chosen because they were the well-educated or because they were in tune with God. All He asks is for us to be willing.

Serve Him in whatever capacity He asks, even if it seems too mediocre or too wild for you. That's what service to God is—doing what He wants, not what we want to do for Him.

Each of us has been created by God in a specific way. We each have characteristics and idiosyncrasies that set us apart from anyone else. While these differences may seem random, they serve a specific purpose.

We each have specific jobs to do for the Lord and those jobs require the specific abilities He has given us. There are some people to whom Alma and I cannot talk, but you can. They will not listen to us; they are tuned to hear your story and your witness.

Just as Mordecai told Esther, "And who knows but that you have come to a royal position for such a time as this?" (Esther 4:14).

I remember when my eyes were more fixed on judging others—what they did and how they acted—than on looking at me and that I was judging. That changed when I found freedom in Christ. Now, it's far easier to love others as they are and how Christ sees them. That is the attitude of service to others—loving.

My daughter Lindsay shared a paper that she wrote for one of her classes at a Christian college. It was on abortions and how we, as a church, frequently abort women in our churches because of the bumper stickers, T-shirts, etc., that speak against abortions.

These slogans and statements truly say much. Yes, God likely is not pleased with abortion, but neither is He pleased with our condemnation of those in favor of abortion. It is not our place. These sayings tell women that they will not be forgiven; they will not be shown grace; and they will not be allowed to heal.

It is interesting to ask people, "Have you reached out to one of these women and said, 'Jesus Christ will forgive you if you ask, and so will I!'?" We need to reach out.

Serving others is bringing together all that we have learned about our Lord and presenting it to them so they too can learn. Serving is comforting, encouraging, building up, strengthening, and much more, all in the way Jesus would have done. Serving is listening, not just hearing; walking beside, not ahead of; and helping, not doing for.

Serving is for the best interests of others, which are not always what they want but what they need. This part is difficult because the carnal spirit has a great desire to get it's own way. Getting our way does not usually or always meet our needs. We sometimes treat symptoms rather than causes.

Symptoms show up and point to a problem. If you have chicken pox on the outside, then you have the associated virus on the inside. A great number of symptoms plague us, and they are all the result of another problem.

Our tendency is to alleviate the discomfort of the symptom and ignore the problem. The problem then continues and often worsens. This same attitude is carried over to other areas of life where symptoms show and problems are ignored, to our detriment.

The apostle Paul said in 1 Corinthians 9:22, "To the weak I became weak, to win the weak. I have become all things to all men so that by all possible means I might save some." We need to become all things to all men as well. It is our job, our purpose in the Lord, to reach out to those who need our help.

Do we need to include admitting we are sinners? Yes, we were sinners, and often, we look as though we never were. People need to see that we were in the same place that they are. We must show that it's possible, through Jesus's sacrifice, to become an heir of the kingdom of God.

Sometimes, we can go too far for our own good. There are times when a Christian sets out to win over the lost on their own turf. Going into a bar to win over the lost can just as easily end up with our being converted to drinkers like them. First, it is just one drink, then another, and so on, until it seems too late for us.

Yes, Jesus hung around with tax collectors and sinners, and yes, we should not shy away from sinners, but we must be careful in our weakness that we are not influenced by them more than they are influenced by us.

Seek to win the lost but not at the expense of being lost again yourself. Be an influence. Don't be influenced.

Becoming a servant of God, taking heed of His voice and direction of service, and being completely in His will is by far the most rewarding place to be. The adventure is like no other. The satisfaction is unlike any other. This comes from being set apart for service to God—being holy.

As I am no longer committed to my own pleasures in life, I now am committed to those of my heavenly Father.

And you?

## FULLNESS OF REPENTANCE:
# THE FINAL CHOICE

You may have made wrong choices along the way, but Christ is the right choice to change things around completely. That choice is going to the throne of God, to the throne of sufficient grace, to the throne of love that can transform you from the inside out and make you into a new creation that's worth acknowledging in the mirror. You then can become a beacon of light to the world because God has touched you.

Is it any wonder I love my Lord? He did what I could not do for myself. And He can do it for you too.

Repentance is a single movement, as described by biblical authors. When Christ spoke of repenting in Luke 13:1–5, it was as one motion from sinfulness to righteousness, from human will to God's will. It is a requirement for the forgiveness of sin (Acts 2:38). The Hebrews writer considers repentance something to happen once and from which to progress.

In this book, *repentance* has been segmented for easier accomplishment, broken into workable stages. Each of these stages is easily recognizable and suits the palate of most people. We have looked at these stages and worked through them. We urge everyone to now mold them back into a single, powerful movement event in their lives. When you change your way, change all the way.

Repentance is the relinquishment of any practice, while under a conviction that it has offended God. You stop doing something because God wants you to stop.

The beginning of repentance can be identified as the moment that remorse for sin sets in. Remorse is the initial form of repentance.

If you remember, in a previous chapter, we talked about remorse, which is a sincere regret for an action we have taken. Without that remorse, there is no repentance.

Remorse is the first instance when individuals realize they are going in a bad direction in their lives. While they may not turn from their actions, they at least recognize their actions are detrimental. This is the birth of repentance in the heart.

> Godly sorrow brings repentance that leads to salvation and leaves no regret, but worldly sorrow brings death. (2 Corinthians 7:10)

The final choice is to not go back to that practice ever again. This may have to be a continual, daily choice, but that is the fullness of repentance—making the better choices stick.

The next level is the recognition of repentance in the mind. This is the time when most commit their lives to the Lord Jesus Christ. It's the time we call repentance, but it is not necessarily the time we lose all desire for the evil.

Following this is a working repentance, which is the time we try to turn all our desires to the will of God. The final stage is when all our intent, all our desire, and all our work is dedicated to the glory of God, according to His good and perfect will. Some call this righteousness, some call it holiness, and some call it perfect in Christ. It is also the time of the *fullness of repentance*, when mind (knowledge), heart (desire), and body (actions) are all involved.

The *fullness of repentance* is the entire process of turning from sin in our own power to righteousness in God's power. This is not by anything we do, only by what God does in and for us (Ephesians 2:9). Perhaps this is a process that takes time, but Christ referred to it as a single moment in time, a crisis moment, a turning point (Luke 13:1–9). Perhaps the process that takes time is getting to this crisis moment.

Whatever length of time it takes you is well worth spending. Go through repentance now. Go through it to its fullness. Do not stop until you arrive at your destination—Christlikeness.

This process may be much slower than reading this book and much more demanding of your attention, but every bit is worth the effort.

When you have reached the fullness of repentance in one area of your life, start in another. When you are able, reach back and help someone else who is early in the process or who has not yet begun. Make this a lifestyle that stays with you.

I dealt with guilt for twenty to twenty-five years for some of the sins I committed in my youth. I was overwhelmed with grief at times. I never—not at any point—decided to continue doing those things I felt sorry for. That is the fullness of repentance.

God's grace was complete way back then, years ago, but I chose to carry the guilt and shame myself.

> But because of his great love for us, God, who is rich in mercy, made us alive with Christ even when we were dead in transgressions—it is by grace you have been saved. (Ephesians 2:4–5)

God's work is complete. God's work is complete for me. God's work is complete for you.

My daughter refreshed my spirit recently when she called and said, "Mom, you will be so proud of me." She said that she had made a decision. "I woke up this morning and decided I was not going to beat myself up anymore for the things I have done wrong. I am a new creation in Christ, and He died for those things, so I am not carrying them anymore."

God said it; I believe it, so let's move on! Amen.

| The Process of Repentance | | | | |
|---|---|---|---|---|
| Sin | Remorse | Repentance | Working Repentance | Righteousness |
| our will | | | | God's will |
| absence of repentance | initial repentance | recognition of repentance | repentance at work | fullness of repentance |
| ← | \ | ↑ | / | → |
| Direction of focus | | | | |

Printed in the United States
by Baker & Taylor Publisher Services